Overcoming Bitterness

GET AWAY FROM ME, SATAN!

To Feida
Blessing in Jesus,
Gwen Mouliert
11-2-02

GWEN MOULIERT

Fire Wind™

Mansfield, PA

ISBN: #1-883906-43-1

Fire Wind
P.O. Box 506
Mansfield, PA 16933

(570) 662-7515
(800) 597-1123

http://www.kingdompub.com
email = info@kingdompub.com

Acknowledgements

The first person who must be acknowledged and thanked is God the Holy Spirit, who gently revealed hidden bitterness in my heart; and I am eternally grateful to the Lord Jesus Christ, for His love and mercy, and for the Father's forgiveness and cleansing.

Next I want to thank my husband, Concepcion, and my children, Mimi and Matthew, for all their encouragement during the years that I have been uncovering roots of bitterness. They never knew what I would unearth next.

To my dear friend Jeannie Sink who prayed for me and with me, as she listened to the sermon on bitter waters dozens and dozens of times and never got bitter with so much repetition.

And a special thanks to Nancy Lambert who did such a wonderful job in the editing of this manuscript, and to Kingdom Publishing for the awesome book you now hold in your hand.

Bondage Exodus 1:14

Sickness Isaiah 38:15-22

Affliction 2 Kings 14:26

Sin Acts 8:23

Injustice Genesis 27:34-38

Marriage Colossians 3:19

Children Proverbs 17:25

Backsliding Jeremiah 2:19

Table of Contents

Preface

Praise the Lord, the book is written. I can't tell you how wonderful I feel to finally have this release. The topic of bitterness affects every Christian sooner or later, and God has been dealing with me on bitterness since the early nineties. His teaching is so exciting, but I think you'll find, as it says in Ecclesiastes, that the end is better than the beginning. The first chapter introduces the concept of "BitterSweet", and we have a long hard way to travel before ending with the "Plague in the Place"—a chapter concerning the prevention of future bitterness.

It is my prayer that God will not only reveal areas in your life, too, where you have held bitterness, but will also work in you mightily to bring forgiveness. May you know the wonderful release that comes when a sinful bondage is broken. Don't we serve an awesome God? Jesus came to set the captives free, and what can I say to that but "Hallelujah! Amen!"

Chapter 1

Bittersweet

"Though you have made me see troubles, many and bitter, you will restore my life again; from the depths of the earth you will again bring me up" (Psalm 71:20, NIV)

How do we become bitter in the first place? Nobody sets out to be bitter. You didn't. I didn't. How do we end up, then, feeling as though bitterness is so strongly rooted in our hearts that it will take a miracle to remove it?

Maybe you're not the one who personally needs this teaching. Perhaps you're reading this book on behalf of a spouse, a child, or a friend who displays bitter feelings regularly. If so, I'd like to shake your hand. You are in a very tiny minority of people who don't wrestle, at one time or another, with bitter feelings. (Don't feel badly if you discover by chapter four or five that you had bitter thoughts that you never before recognized. Just be glad the Lord directed you to this teaching!)

How can so many Christians suffer from bitterness? We might expect worldly unbelievers to wrestle with bitterness. After all, they haven't found the joy of a personal Savior and are still on a mission to fix everything by themselves. If they can't get the job done in one lifetime, they assume they can just hang on for a few more. (That's a pretty major assumption!) Some try to hold the belief that man is basically good. If so, there could be a lot of bitterness in having to keep adjusting that word *good* to encompass abortion, gang violence, and biological warfare. But rather than itemize the reasons for the lost to feel bitter, let's return to our question about Christians being bitter. In order to find the answer, we have to review the concept I call *BitterSweet*.

You've heard of things being bittersweet, and yet we sometimes wonder how these two words can be linked together. Aren't they in opposition to one another? It's like so many other common oxymorons: *jumbo shrimp*, *pretty ugly*, and even *same difference*. Same difference? Does that make any sense? Probably it makes as much sense as bittersweet, yet there are many times in the Bible when the Word of God uses bitter and sweet in conjunction.

Bitterness Defined

Let's define bitter and sweet to see if we're missing something. The word *bitter* refers to an unpleasant taste, something sharp or acrid. This is in contrast to *sweet*, which by definition is pleasing to the taste, having an agreeable smell or appearance. *Bitter* has other meanings apart from taste, but I'd like to show you a passage in Scripture that deals specifically with bitter and sweet tastes.

> *"And the voice which I heard from heaven spake unto me again, and said, Go and take the little book which is open in the hand of the angel which standeth upon the sea and upon the earth.*
> *And I went unto the angel, and said unto him, Give me the little book. And he said unto me, Take it, and eat it up; and it shall make thy belly bitter, but it shall be in thy mouth sweet as honey.*
> *And I took the little book out of the angel's hand, and ate it up; and it*

was in my mouth sweet as honey: and as soon as I had eaten it, my belly was bitter.
And he said unto me, Thou must prophesy again before many peoples, and nations, and tongues, and kings"   (Revelation 10:8-11).

Sweet in the mouth, bitter in the belly. That's an interesting concept. It reminds me of the semisweet or bittersweet chocolate chips. They are supposed to be used in recipes for baking. If you're like me, when you prepared a delicious dessert with these morsels, you just had to drop a few in your mouth. Actually, if you're like me, those few soon became *many*. I never had to worry about chocolate melting in my hand because it was transferred into my belly with the speed of light. It's so easy to binge on chocolate. It's sweet in the mouth, but after overindulgence, it certainly makes for a bitter belly.

So it is with life. When something that was once sweet turns bitter, we will be overheard using phrases like these: "What a bitter pill to swallow" or "It has left such a bitter taste in my mouth." And when pain or tragedy afflicts us or those we love, we may ask why we had to drink from such "a *bitter* cup."

Marah, an Old Testament Word

A study of the Old Testament reveals that the ancient Hebrews used similar expressions. They would often describe tragedy or other unpleasant experiences in terms of the sense of taste, calling something bitter or galling. Surely bitterness, then, falls into the category of universal human experience.

There are several different words in the Hebrew language that are translated bitter or bitterness, but the one that seems to be the most frequently used is the word *marah*. Checking *Strong's Concordance*[1] and also the *Theological Wordbook of the Old Testament,*[2] we find the following definition for *marah*: chafed, angry, discontented, heavy. Wow! Those are some aspects to bitterness that we may not have considered. Let's take a closer look at each one.

Chafe *means to make warm, to make sore by rubbing and irritating, to annoy, to rub against, thus causing anger.*
Some definitions for angry *include tight, constricted, painfully inflamed.*
Discontented *has to do with a lack of contentment, obviously, but also being restless, and having a desire for something else.*
Heavy *means hard to lift or move because it is weighty.*

Don't these definitions give us a clearer picture of the word *bitter?* When we have bitter things happen in our lives, we must guard against being irritated and annoyed. If those emotions are given free rein, we will become angry and then discontented and restless. We may also sense a spirit of heaviness resting on us, finding the bitterness more of a burden than we can bear or can remove by ourselves.

The Bible shares many accounts of people who dealt with bitterness or *marah.* We're going to touch on several in order to see what kinds of situations provoked bitterness, and then we'll look at how the response of bitterness was turned bittersweet.

One such story is told in the very first book of the Bible, Genesis. A vivid word picture is given to us in chapter 27: The great patriarch Isaac is on his deathbed and wants to impart the blessing to his oldest son, Esau. Jacob, not the firstborn, came in disguised as his older brother and stole the blessing, which was a double portion. We can easily see Esau's wrath at finding that his blessing is gone, conveyed instead to his younger brother.

> *"And when Esau heard the words of his father, he cried with a great and exceeding bitter cry, and said unto his father, Bless me, even me also, O my father"* (Genesis 27:34).

Esau experienced *marah* in his very own home. How bitter it is when we are wounded, hurt, and betrayed by our very own family members! Aren't they the ones who are supposed to love us the most? How can they be so selfish? (On the other hand, haven't we also been guilty of selfishness and lack of love? Shouldn't we reflect a bit, with the help of the Holy

Spirit, on our own actions and motives?)

Marah on Behalf of a People

Another Biblical account that uses the word *marah* is in the wonderful book of Esther. This book takes place in Persia, when the Medes and Persians controlled most of the known world. We only get as far as chapter 2 when we meet a very godly man named Mordecai. He is a Jewish man, living in Persia, who has adopted and raised his niece, Esther. She is frankly described as fair and beautiful. Before long, Esther is taken into the palace of the King and ends up winning a royal beauty pageant. (Women can really relate to the beauty regimen described in this book: six months of oil massages and six months of different perfumes and cosmetics. Whew!) Esther not only wins the pageant; she wins the heart of the king and becomes his new queen.

Now, the king doesn't know that she is a Hebrew. She has kept her nationality a secret in the palace, and her Uncle Mordecai is the only one who knows she was a Jew. This is significant because of an evil man named Haman, who at this time has been trying to destroy the Jews. Haman has a significant influence upon the king, having been promoted above all the other princes of the land. At Haman's request, the king writes a law to have all the Jews annihilated. Mordecai discovers this pending destruction of God's people, and the Bible vividly describes his bitter state.

> *"When Mordecai perceived all that was done, Mordecai rent his clothes, and put on sackcloth with ashes, and went out into the midst of the city, and cried with a loud and a bitter cry"* (Esther 4:1).

Can you relate to Mordecai's feelings? He was in a place of *marah* because of the injustice of others and their hatred of his kinsmen.

We're going to leave Mordecai for the moment and turn to one of the most famous of Bible characters, Job. Even those who haven't read the Bible have heard of Job. His name has come to stand for one who has suffered greatly, but he didn't start out that way.

Marah from Profound Loss

Job was a righteous man, the Bible tells us, who loved God and avoided evil. God was so proud of his faithful servant that he even bragged about him on a day when the angels of God appeared before His throne, and Satan also appeared there in heaven. (Does this surprise you as much as it does me? This was after Satan's rebellion and defeat, when he and one-third of the angels were cast out of heaven. In Revelation 12:7-11 you'll find another account of that event and the spiritual warfare involved.)

The Lord actually asked the devil if he had considered Job. This started a whole series of problems, particularly because even though the devil did consider Job, Job didn't consider the devil. Since Job couldn't see into the heavenly realms, he was clueless as to the challenge about to take place.

Satan slyly remarked that Job only obeyed God because of all the blessings he had received. Indeed Job was blessed. He had 10 children, good health, and great wealth. The devil suggested that if Job were afflicted, he would curse God fast enough. God accepted the challenge and allowed the devil to attack Job. What an attack that was!

Finances, possessions, and children were all involved in the enemy's first onslaught. Job's response was to tear his robe, shave his head, and fall down upon the ground, worshipping God. He said, *"Naked came I out of my mother's womb, and naked shall I return thither: the LORD gave, and the LORD hath taken away; blessed be the name of the LORD"* (Job 2:21).

Once again Satan appeared with the angels before the throne of God. This time he asserted that Job would surely curse God if he suffered physically. God permitted the next attack, putting the restriction that Job's life was to be spared. By the time Satan had finished afflicting Job's flesh with boils, Job was sorry there was such a restriction. His own wife advised him to curse God and die. However, even though Job experienced great bitterness, he remained a man of integrity and didn't curse God. He had to ask a question, though, that is in the heart of many of us when we have troubles. *"Wherefore is light given to him that is in misery, and life unto the bitter in soul"* (Job 3:20).

Have you ever been bitter in your soul? Many times, when we don't have the light needed to see the real issue at stake in our lives, we can become bitter to the point where we have bitterness toward God. Had Job really been given light, he would have had the vision and insight to discern this was a spiritual fight, not just a set of natural tragedies.

Poor Job had lost his health, along with his wealth. His children had been killed in a terrible accident while they gathered at Job's eldest son's home to celebrate his birthday. Job was in so much pain and sorrow that he even accused the Lord of this being from His hand.

Misery and bitterness of soul can cause us to shift our focus. This is the real danger. We lose sight of our Savior and see only our problems and misfortunes. With our perceptions distorted we tend to misplace blame. Although Job had been a godly man, he cried out, *"The arrows of the Almighty are within me, the poison whereof drinketh up my spirit: the terrors of God do set themselves in array against me"* (Job 6:4). The book clearly says that these arrows were from the devil, although God permitted this. The New Testament also tells us to be on guard against the weapons of the enemy—even calling them fiery darts or arrows. Indeed, the arrows that struck Job and his family were not the arrows of the Almighty but of the serpent.

We need to take a closer look at the imagery Job used. He said *"the poison whereof drinketh up my spirit."* Bitterness is the real poison to our spirits. Have you ever been poisoned like Job, bitter with the difficult and tragic things you've experienced? So many times we blame God for the workings of the devil. Job's bitterness seems intensified because he thought God had brought all of these calamities about. Have you also experienced a *marah* like this toward the Father?

The Marah of Loneliness

There was a woman in the Bible who declared that her very name should be *Mara* because of the things she had endured.. Her real name was Naomi, which means "pleasantness" and "joyful one." Instead, she was very bitter toward God. (You can read her story in the book of Ruth. I can relate to Naomi, but when we have bittersweet experiences in life if we don't try to remain sweet, bitterness will settle in us. At that point, we don't even approach being pleasant, let alone joyful.

Naomi, her husband, and their two sons lived in Bethlehem of Judah. A famine hit their region and they decided to move to the land of Moab. While in Moab, Naomi's husband died. (Can you even imagine being in a foreign country and losing your mate?)

Her sons had married women from Moab, but Naomi sounds as though she still clung to her sons closely. Yet, both her sons became ill and died. It is hard to picture what Naomi must have felt. She was in a distant land, far from the familiar things and the neighbors that might have brought her some comfort.

In her misery, she said the hand of the Lord was against her. She complained that the Almighty had dealt very bitterly with her. Had He indeed done as she accused, or was her grief so heavy that she assumed even God was against her? Naomi thought of herself as *Mara* because of her grief at losing those she loved. She felt empty, without purpose, and totally alone.

Can you remember a tragedy or death that caused you to blame God? Did you ever feel that joy had completely left your life? Has loneliness been a bitter companion? We can see how sweet hope would be, by contrast, in this kind of life situation. If we could only believe...

The Marah of Unfulfilled Desires

Another woman in the Bible who wept because of her circumstances is Hannah. Hannah wasn't in bitterness because of a death, but rather because she could not produce life. She was barren. Her story is found in the book of First Samuel.

Hannah was married to a man named Elkanah, a name which means "one whom God possesses." Even though Elkanah was possessed of God, there was someone else who also possessed him. That someone was his other wife, Peninnah. Hannah's husband was not the cause of her infertility because he also had children with Penninah.

Hannah didn't know that the Lord had closed her womb, and she desperately wanted to have a child. She became very bitter at her barrenness. The bittersweet aspect of her situation is poignant. She and her husband really loved one another, so she must have been pleased for him that he had children. She was bitter, though, that the children were by another woman.

Her disappointment that God had not granted the desires of her heart was mixed with the feeling that His Word was not being fulfilled in her life either. Didn't the Word of God say to be fruitful and multiply?

Can you relate to this kind of bitter disappointment? Sometimes we blame another person for our disappointments, but we know in our hearts that we are really bitter toward God. There are times that we pray, seeking something we want that is in God's Word, yet we don't receive the promise in the manner or fashion we wanted. Our disappointment increases when we see others receiving all around us, while we remain barren.

We read in 1 Samuel 1 that when Hannah arrived in the house of God, she was in bitterness of soul. She prayed to the Lord and "wept sore." But we read later that in His timing, God opened her womb and blessed a nation.

How many times have we wept with disappointment over the timing of God's promises? God has a plan, though, to remove the infertility and allow His seed to reproduce His likeness in our hearts and lives.

Marah and Murmuring

We must look at one more person who had to deal not only with disappointment over God's timing, but a whole nation of people who were bitter against the Lord. (See Exodus.) God had used Moses in a mighty and magnificent way to bring the people of God out of their Egyptian bondage. For many years they had known only slavery, but finally they walked into freedom. It took ten plagues for Pharaoh to let the Hebrews go, but all of Egypt saw the awesome power of Jehovah demonstrated again and again. After seeing the miracles performed on their behalf, how could the Jews be bitter?

The answer is that their memories for miracles became short when their circumstances grew difficult in the wilderness. We can hardly believe it, but it wasn't long before they began to murmur and complain to Moses. There are few things that open the door to a spirit of bitterness like murmuring and complaining.

Just think! They were fed supernaturally everyday. The bread of heaven fell for them to gather. They called it manna, which means, "what is it?" (And until we get to heaven, we won't know what it is, either.)

Taking a giant leap to the end of the Bible, we find in the book of Revelation that it is the overcoming church which gets to eat of the hidden manna. Backing up to Psalms 78, we discover in verse 25 that manna was the "bread of the angels." Doesn't this sound like it must be good? It is a fact, however, that when we complain about God's provision, we allow bitterness to enter our lives. We become unable to recognize how good the gifts of God really are.

The Hebrew people came to Moses and complained about the manna. They wanted meat. (I can't help thinking of the commercial a few years back where an older woman kept demanding, "Where's the beef!") Moses knew he couldn't provide meat to feed over a million people, and he allowed some *marah* to enter his own soul.

His story, found in Numbers chapter eleven, relates that in his bitterness, he asked the Lord why He had afflicted him with the burden of all these complaining people. Moses went so far as to say, "*If thou deal thus with me, kill me, I pray thee, out of hand*" (Numbers 11:15a).

However, it wasn't God's will to kill Moses—the complainers yes, but Moses no. Instead, He intervened and sent laborers to lift the burden from Moses (Numbers 11:16,17). Personally, I think God sent help to Moses because Moses was so honest concerning his bitterness toward a people who had forgotten how God delivered them from bondage. What happened to their trust and faith? It didn't last long, did it? Does ours? How many of us would have the courage to speak to the Lord in the frank fashion Moses used?

Marah and Burnout

Today, many of us in leadership find ourselves "dying" not only because of bitterness and resentment we develop toward those we lead, but also because we are too proud to admit to God that we need help. We are often too concerned with our Christian image to admit that we are actually feeling emotions like *bitterness and resentment*. We keep telling each other that we are "fine, just fine, thanks," until the day that we resign, overcome by the weight of our burdens. Can you relate to not having enough time or ability to meet the demands made on you? Those in leadership especially find there are just too many people with too many problems. There aren't enough hours in a day to lift their burdens, let alone find help for our own needs.

Please be assured that as the Lord sent help to Moses, so He will send you someone to help lift the burden you bear. Our responsibility is to be as open, honest, and direct with the Lord as Moses was when he began to feel bitterness of heart. He knows how you feel anyway, so why try to hide it from Him? Come to Him expectantly, knowing that He has the answers and He is good.

A Place Called Marah

There is another point in Scripture when the people of God put terrible demands on Moses with their complaining. This is the time that they were lacking water. It's ironic, isn't it, that the first plague had to do with God turning the water of Egypt into blood? It is even more ironic that these same people had seen God's hand first holding back the waters of the Red Sea so they could pass through dry-shod, and then releasing a flood that drowned the Egyptian army. At the time, the people celebrated this miraculous deliverance with tambourines and singing. Miriam and the women sang praises to God, *"...the horse and his rider hath he thrown into the sea"* (Exodus 15:21).

Only three days after this mighty victory, they entered the desert and began to wish they had some water. What they found was a place of bitter waters, which they named Marah. What could they do? They had traveled three days into the wilderness of Shur and now the only water they had to drink was contaminated. It's interesting that the word *Shur* means "a wall." The Hebrew people had hit a wall and without divine intervention, they were sure to die of thirst.

Their cry of *marah* soon became a great murmuring. You can live for many days without food, but you can't survive without fluids; and in the desert, water vanishes very quickly. Once again they cried out for Moses to do something. He had held out his staff at the Red Sea. Couldn't he extend his staff again over this pool and make it pure?

Moses wasn't about to do anything the Lord hadn't told him to do. Instead, he sought the face of God. There are a few lessons in this for us. For example, faith is a wonderful thing as long as it isn't presumption. God is not a God of formulas. We can rejoice in what He did for us yesterday, but we are to seek God for each day's needs and for answers to life's problems. We can't live on the strength of yesterday's "quiet time." We must daily acknowledge our dependence upon Him. He who has promised will be faithful to provide His presence and His plan for each situation, when we ask Him.

There is another important lesson to be learned from the example of Moses. As the story continues, we find that Moses did indeed hear the instruction from the Lord. It was a plan, though, that demanded obedience. God told Moses to cast a tree into the bitter waters. Even though this sounded like a strange solution, Moses knew better than to doubt. Because Moses was a man who trusted God, He obeyed and found that the bitter waters were made sweet. When we trust God, seek Him, and obey His instructions, we will find our bitter areas of life becoming sweet as well.

It is a fact that all of us will encounter bitterness in our lives. We sometimes won't know a pool of water is bitter until we taste it. We may see a solution ahead of us, as the children of Israel saw the pool of water in the desert. We try to apply the solution, as they tried to drink the water, only to find that it simply won't work. Thanks be to God that we have a Deliverer. As we encounter *marah* and pools of bitter waters in our lives, we need to be like Moses and cry out to God. He will not only heal the bitter waters but also establish Himself as *"the Lord that healeth thee"* (Exodus 15:26*b*).

If left untreated, the bitterness in our hearts will produce sickness. Many times this will develop into an actual physical illness, but certainly emotional and spiritual sickness will be experienced. The only way to make these painful, bitter experiences and problems have any sweetness to them is to put "the tree into a pool." After all, this was God's explicit instruction to Moses. If he would put the tree into the bitter waters, God would then be the Lord their physician. When hurts, wounds, and life bitterness have affected us to the point of illness, we definitely need to turn to the Lord as our healer.

But how do we put a tree into a pool for healing? Not by a tree in the hand of Moses, but through the tree of the Lord called Calvary. Jesus willingly accepted the curse of being hung on a tree so that we could receive the blessing of forgiveness of sins and life everlasting. If we will bring to the cross our bitterness and the pools of pain in our hearts, Jesus will remove the sting from the bitter *marahs*. The next time you are in the wilderness and come to a pool of *marah* in your life, do what Moses did. Cry out to the Lord, and see if He doesn't prove Himself *the Lord that healeth thee.*

From Bitter to Sweet

Let's take a look at those mentioned previously in this chapter. Each supplies an example of one who allowed the Lord to turn the bitterness in life to the sweet.

Esau eventually forgave his brother Jacob. What a wonderful healing these family members experienced as the figurative tree was applied to their wounds and hurts. (See Genesis 33: 4-11.) Jesus can help us to forgive even those close family members who have repeatedly hurt us and left us bitter. As we look to His example, we see that even as He died on the tree, Jesus said, "Father, forgive them. They know not what they do" (Luke 23:32).

In the story of Esther, Mordecai became an instrument of deliverance for the household of faith. He had a bitter enemy against him, but that enemy was defeated. On the brink of national disaster, Mordecai had sought God in faith and obeyed all of His instructions. In consequence, the people of God were saved, and Mordecai was given a giant promotion. In our own perplexities, we too must seek God and obey Him.

Job gives us insight on the importance of wholehearted and humble repentance. He received a double portion of blessing as a result.

Naomi was honest concerning her bitter feelings. Her cries to God for deliverance were heard, and she became part of the lineage of King David.

Hannah, who also sought God fervently, became the mother of Samuel, a great prophet in the Old Testament.

With God's help, we can forgive as Esau did. We can repent as Job did. We can be delivered, then restored, and promoted, as Mordecai was. Best of all, because the Lord Jesus conquered sin and death on the tree of Calvary, we who have received Him as Savior and Lord have been adopted into His family. Our lineage now reveals God as our Father. *"But as many as received him, to them gave he power to become the sons of God, even to them that believe on his name: Which were born, not of blood, nor of the will of the flesh, nor of the will of man, but of God"* (John 1:12,13).

Finally, we learn that through His obedience and loyalty to God, Moses was called God's friend. Jesus tells us in the New Testament, *"Ye are my friends, if ye do whatsoever I command you. Henceforth I call you not servants; for the servant knoweth not what his lord doeth: but I have called you friends; for all things that I have heard of my Father I have made known unto you"* (John 15:14,15).

There is no power in bitterness to bind us if we submit each event of our lives to the transforming power of the cross. In fact, the Word tells us to go a step farther. *"Count it all joy, my brethren, when you meet various trials, for you know that the testing of your faith produces steadfastness. And let steadfastness have its full effect, that you may be perfect and complete, lacking in nothing"* (James 1:2-4).

The question each of us must ask ourselves it this: Are we bitter because of what we have gone through, or have these difficult events made us better? If we look closely at these two words, *bitter* and *better*, we see there is only one letter that needs transformation—and that is the letter "I."

For Reflection
1. Do any of the synonyms for *marah* strike a chord with you—chafed, angry discontented, or heavy?

2. Have you had bitter situations with family members? Felt bitter due to injustice, personal tragedy, loneliness, or unfulfilled desires?

3. Have you struggled with bitterness brought on by the complaining or demands of others? Your own expectations of yourself? Simple burnout?

4. When you look at Jesus rather than your problems, what happens? Who do you blame for your "trials"?

5. When is faith *not* faith but *presumption*?

6. Why does God permit us to go through difficult things?

Endnotes

1. *Strong's Exhaustive Concordance of the Bible* (Hendrickson Publishers; Peabody, Mass.)

2. Definitions from the *Theological Wordbook of the Old Testament* by R. Harris; Gleason Archer, Jr.; and Bruce K. Waltke.

Bitter Waters

Everyone knows that water is a mainstay for our lives. We can live without food for many days, but we cannot exist without water or some type of fluid because our bodies are actually made up of 80% water! Many times when we are hot or tired, we try drinking a lot of different things to quench our thirst, but to no avail. The drink that works the best and gets the job done is plain, old-fashioned H_2O.

The Bible has much to say about water, but perhaps the most positive and intriguing references are to *living water*. We find this phrase seven times in Scripture, and each time it is a descriptive phrase referring to God Himself, in one or the other persons of the trinity. In the book of John we find Jesus saying, *"'Whoever believes in me, as the Scripture has said, streams of living water will flow from within him.'"* (John 7:38) This is an amazing statement. John explains in the next verse, *"By this he meant the Spirit, whom those who believed in him were later to receive"* (39a). Living water sounds like something that is extra desirable for life. We certainly wouldn't want to drink something called dead water or dying water. (The fact that there are resorts along the Dead Sea never ceases to amaze me. It seems so contradictory.)

Water from a Rock?

Some amazing accounts of God's provision of living water are found in the book of Exodus. Are you familiar with the story in Exodus 17 of Moses getting water from a rock? Let's check out a few verses to appreciate this story.

> *"And all the congregation of the children of Israel journeyed from the wilderness of Sin* [isn't *that* interesting], *after their journeys, according to the commandment of the Lord, and pitched in Rephidim: and there was no water for the people to drink.*
> *Wherefore the people did chide with Moses, and said, Give us water that we may drink. And Moses said unto them, Why chide ye with me? Wherefore do ye tempt the Lord?*
> *And the people thirsted there for water; and the people murmured against Moses, and said, Wherefore is this that thou has brought us up out of Egypt, to kill us and our children and our cattle with thirst?"*
> (Exodus 17:1-3)

The people are desperate for water. Ironically or prophetically, *Rephidim* comes from a Hebrew root which implies rest and refreshment.[1] The people don't stop with simply complaining, though. In the next verses, Moses cries out to God that the people are about to stone him. God then gives these instructions to Moses:

> *"Go on before the people and take with thee of the elders of Israel; and thy rod, wherewith thou smotest the river, take in thine hand, and go. Behold, I will stand before thee there upon the rock in Horeb; and thou shalt smite the rock, and there shall come water out of it, that the people may drink. And Moses did so in the sight of the elders of Israel."* (Exodus 17:5,6)

The name *Horeb* comes from a root meaning "to parch through drought" and by extension "to make desolate, destroy, or kill." When Moses smote that rock, everything was changed. In the New Testament, we are told that Christ is the rock, and because He was smitten for us the waters of God come to refresh us.

"Moreover, Brethren, I would not that ye should be ignorant, how that all our fathers were under the cloud, and all passed through the sea; And were all baptized unto Moses in the cloud and in the sea; And did all eat the same spiritual meat; And did all drink the same spiritual drink: for they drank of that spiritual Rock that followed them: and that Rock was Christ." (1 Corinthians 10:1-4)

When we have dryness in our lives, we also need to go to the rock at Horeb. For Moses, this had been a place of communion with God when he turned aside to see the burning bush. (This miracle is found in Exodus 3 and 4.) I have found that when I am in a very dry wilderness, once I commune with Jesus my Rock, I am refreshed by the living waters He supplies.

There is another event where Moses struck a rock, but this one is surrounded by a very urgent and terrible warning to us. In chapter 20 we read that God instructed Moses and his brother, Aaron, to speak to the rock in order to supply water for the Hebrews. Moses disobeyed God's instructions. Instead of speaking to the rock, he struck it twice. Yes, water did come out of the rock, but God was angry with Moses. Although we often think this anger was provoked solely by Moses' disobedience, there is something else that transpired in this story which is a key and vital element.

When Moses approached the people, he said, *"Must we fetch you water out of this rock?"* (Numbers 20:10)—as though he and Aaron could cause water to come out of a rock. As a matter of fact, when the Lord rebuked Moses for this He said, *"Because ye believed me not, to sanctify me in the eyes of the children of Israel, therefore ye shall not bring this congregation into the land which I have given them"* (Numbers 20:12). Moses wasn't able to enter the Promised Land because of his arrogant remark. This should cause us to be ever so careful that we don't take any credit for the things He has done and is doing in our lives. Clearly, anytime we think that it is our ability, our talent, or our merit that can produce a miracle, we will not be able to enter the Land of Promise. We must always seek to sanctify and glorify God.

Interestingly enough, the place at which this occurred was called *Kadesh*, which is from a root meaning "sanctuary."[2] God desires to set us apart for holy communion with Him, but arrogance obviously breaks that communion. So also, does bitterness. Until the bitterness is removed from our lives, we miss out on the communion, the blessings, and the living water God would impart to us.

In addition to living water, the Bible speaks of other kinds of water—specifically, bitter water. Bitter water doesn't sound too pleasant for drinking; in fact, the Bible shares some really urgent warnings about the poisonous effects of bitter water. We have already taken a brief look in the first chapter at the account of Moses and the people of Israel at the pool of bitter waters they named Marah. Because of the danger presented by this bitter water, we would do well to take a closer look at the details surrounding this event. And while we're doing that, let's examine some of the other "watery" episodes in the life of Moses.

A Brief History of Moses

Scholars tell us that Moses was born around 1500 B.C. in a time of tremendous persecution for the Jews. A Pharaoh who did not know the significance of Joseph was now on the throne. He only knew that the descendants of Joseph had multiplied at such a rate that they were becoming a royal pain in the neck. His Plan A was to make the Jews his slaves, and he made their bondage very bitter. Plan A didn't reduce the Jewish population as much as he hoped, so he moved to Plan B: all the boy babies born to Hebrew women were to be killed.

Praise be to God that there were midwives who feared God more than they feared Pharaoh, and they found excuses not kill the male babies. However, when Pharaoh found out that the midwives were not killing the newborns, he ordered all the little Hebrew baby boys under the age of two to be cast into the river and drowned.

Now Moses' mother was a God-fearing woman who was blessed with great resourcefulness. For the first three months of his life, she hid Moses from the Egyptians. That in itself could have been no easy task. Babies are not exactly the quietest of all God's creatures. Can you imagine what this woman went through?

"I thought I just heard a baby cry?"

"A baby? No, I didn't hear any baby. I've been having a lot of indigestion lately, though. Must have been my stomach rumbling from all those leeks and onions…"

Seriously though, the Word tells us that when his mother could hide him no longer, she made an ark for Moses and set him afloat on the river. She also sent his older sister, Miriam, to watch over Moses and report back what happened to him. I wonder if it was a shock to her or if she planned to float her baby in the direction of Pharaoh's daughter, who evidently bathed in the Nile on a regular basis. The princess had no children and her biological clock was ticking. She adopted the baby and named him Moses, meaning to rescue and draw out of water; so already there were several connections with Moses and water—potentially bitter experiences, too—but that's only the beginning.

Pharaoh's daughter raised Moses in all the tradition of the Egyptians, but at some point along the way, Moses figured out that he was really a Hebrew. (Perhaps his birth mother, who just happened to be on hand to serve as his nurse, told him.) As an adult, one day he saw a fellow Hebrew being mistreated by an Egyptian, and so Moses murdered the Egyptian. In fear, he hid the body in the sand. The next day, though, when he tried to stop a couple of Hebrews from fighting with each other, they let him know that the murder was not exactly a secret. Rather than see him as an ally, the Hebrews figured he just liked to kill people and asked if he was going to kill them, too! Fearing retribution, Moses fled for his own life into the desert. That had to be a terribly difficult time for Moses. He lived in the middle of an identity crisis—not fully accepted by either the Egyptians or the Hebrews.

After many years in the burning sands, Moses was confronted by the voice of God coming from a bush ablaze in the wilderness. Isn't it a comfort for us to know that even when people sin and try to cover their tracks—even when they think they have escaped—they are not invisible to the eye of God? It's an even greater comfort that God can still use us after the sins and mistakes we have made. What a God of love! After Moses kills a man, God speaks to Moses and uses him to tell people, "Thou shalt not kill." Moses wasn't speaking out of hypocrisy. He had truly been changed by the living God.

Let My People Go!

The Lord then sent Moses to Pharaoh as a deliverer for the children of God. Although Moses was reluctant at first, in obedience to God he went to Pharaoh on behalf of the Hebrew children that were in the bondage of slavery. With God prompting him, Moses asked Pharaoh to let the Hebrews go. Most of us are more familiar with this part of the story. Pharaoh had a great thing going with all this free labor and refused to release the Hebrews. Repeatedly, in fact, he hardened his heart to God as well as to Moses. You may have seen this part of the story in the blockbuster movie, *The Ten Commandments*. Well, God eventually did give ten commandments, but first He sent ten plagues.*

It was the tenth plague, the death of the firstborn, that finally convinced Pharaoh to let the people of God go. Yet, after their deliverance from Egypt, Pharaoh once again hardened his heart and reneged on his word. He went after the Hebrew men and women to bring them once again into bondage.

Moses and his people had gone from Succoth (which means "tents")

---

*It would help you to stop at this point and read the account of the plagues in Exodus. The plagues are described in chapters seven through thirteen, but you might want to begin in chapter one of Exodus to fully appreciate what led up to the plagues. In chapter fourteen, the miracle of the Red Sea Crossing is recounted.

and had them camp in Etham—which means "Sea-bound." God was leading them in the wilderness by a pillar of cloud during the day and a pillar of fire by night. They just followed as He directed, and they didn't realize that when they left Etham, they really *were* sea-bound! As Pharaoh began his chase to recapture them, the Hebrews arrived at the Red Sea.

Let's reflect on this for just a moment. Remember that the first plague involved all the rivers—in fact, all the water in Egypt—turning into blood. What they would have seen at that point was a sea of red—all the rivers, ponds, lakes, etc., turned red by God's power. It seems particularly significant that they were once again facing a red river or a red sea. (It's also significant for our discussion that these were definitely bitter water experiences for the Egyptians!)

The Hebrew people lost all the trust they had in Moses and God. They asked Moses if there weren't enough graves in Egypt that he had to lead them out into the wilderness to die. But Moses didn't lose faith. He prophesied a mighty deliverance by a mighty God. When he asked God what the next step would be, God instructed Moses to extend his rod over the Red Sea and to divide it. As he stretched out his arm, the Lord sent a strong east wind to part the sea and dry the ground for the children of Israel. The waters were so divided that they were a wall unto the Hebrews on the right and left hand. Thus another miracle involving water was provided.

Keep in mind that the Egyptians were still following them. Once the Hebrews had passed through the waters, Moses was told to extend his rod once again. This time the waters of the Red Sea came back together. The waters crashed over and drowned all of the enemy right in front of the children of Israel.

Some people have had long discussions pertaining to the depth of the Red Sea. Some have even said the Hebrews wouldn't have had much trouble crossing because the Red Sea was only three inches deep. I guess they ignore the part about crossing dryshod. Maybe they think it was a poetic exaggeration to call the three inches of water on each side a "wall of water." If they're right, I can only say that this is even more of a miracle than we have been led to believe because soldiers and their horses were drowned in only three inches of water! Can you picture this? My guess is the army would hold their horses' heads under the water until they drowned, then they each committed suicide in only three inches of water. Quite a picture! However deep the sea was, the real issue is what God did for His children by delivering them after years of bitter bondage.

Can we even begin to comprehend the joy these people had over their miraculous deliverance? The Hebrew people celebrated this wonder with songs and victory dances—and keep in mind, there were over one million people involved in this celebration. The closest I can come to picturing this is that great day of celebration in the United States when in 1976 we enjoyed our Bi-Centennial year. Do you remember all the preparation and celebration that swept through the land? Every small town had its parade, every city its fireworks. If you think *we* partied to celebrate 200 years of nationhood, you should have been at the crossing of the Red Sea when all the enemies were absolutely defeated and drowned right in front of the children of Israel. Moses burst out with a new chorus, *"I will sing unto the Lord, for He hath triumphed gloriously; the horse and the rider hath He thrown into the sea"* (Exodus 15).

Miriam, Moses' sister, answered his song with great enthusiasm. In verses 20 and 21 of Exodus 15, we read about Miriam and the women dancing and singing. I could wish the chapter and this story had ended in such a high fashion: victory, deliverance, and the awesome assurance that the slavery was ended.

Healing for Bitterness

The very next event that takes place involves the pool of water we discussed briefly in chapter one. The children of Israel had traveled for three days beyond the Red Sea. Up to this point, they had nothing to drink, but suddenly their salvation seemed in view as they came upon a pool of water. Pool sounds small to us, but it couldn't have been that small. There would be well over two million people drinking from it, as well as all of their livestock. Yet when they tried to drink the water, they discovered that it was not life-bringing. You remember that they called it Marah because of the bitterness of the water. *They disregarded all the wonderful miracles they had already observed and reverted to their normal behavior of complaining, murmuring, and crying* for Moses to do something. What did they expect him to do? Thank God that Moses knew his only recourse was to call upon the Lord.

You read about Moses' instructions in our first chapter: the Lord showed Moses a tree and instructed him to cast the tree into the bitter waters. Suddenly the waters were turned sweet, but that's not all:

> *"There the LORD made a decree and a law for them, and there he tested them. He said, "If you listen carefully to the voice of the LORD your God and do what is right in his eyes, if you pay attention to his commands and keep all his decrees, I will not bring on you any of the diseases I brought on the Egyptians, for I am the LORD, who heals you." Then they came to Elim, where there were twelve springs and seventy palm trees, and they camped there near the water"*
> (Exodus 15:22b-27).

Notice that not only did God make provision for the healing of the waters, but the Lord identifies Himself as Jehovah Rapha, the Lord our Physician. He will heal us and not allow the diseases of the Egyptians to come upon us. This promise delights my spirit and my soul because I hate to be sick—disease distresses me. Notice the real extent of this promise, though. Sometimes we think of disease as only attacking our physical bodies. I have come to realize that anytime I have a problem that brings *disease* into my life, I need to be healed. I would have expected Him to make such a promise, though, when sick people were coming to Him with their infirmities, diseases, injuries, and illnesses. It took many years for me to understand why the Lord made such a powerful promise of healing in this setting.

We get a clue in another scriptural passage, concerning His powerful promise in this context. In the Psalms we find this description: *"He brought them forth also with silver and gold; and there was not one feeble person among their tribes"* (Psalm 105:37).

Not one feeble…what could this mean? Doesn't it seem reasonable that after all the years of being mistreated and overworked that surely there were many sick, malnourished, and feeble folks? The word *feeble* means "to falter, be weak, or to stumble." How could this great multitude of people,[3] over two million strong—considering men, women, and children—leave Egypt and not one among them be weak or sickly? Could it be that they received the strength they needed for this wilderness experience on the night before they left their bondage?

Think about it. As the death angel was instructed to kill the firstborn in each house, the children of Israel were kept safe by the blood that had been applied to the doors of their homes. Inside these protected walls, God's people ate the very first Passover meal, a celebration that has been observed throughout every generation since. In partaking of the Passover Lamb and applying the blood of the Lamb, could they have received healing virtue? It's my belief that the Hebrews were healed as well as delivered on that great night so many centuries ago.

If this is true, they received the strength and health they needed to begin their travels on the Passover night; but then they arrived at the bitter waters and were told that God would be their healer. Again, why would He make such a promise of healing in this setting? It makes sense when we understand that bitterness can cause sickness.

A Bitter Curse

This, too, is documented in the Old Testament. The fifth chapter of Numbers contains a lengthy description of the purity of questionable women being diagnosed through the use of bitter waters. The priest had to give bitter waters as a drink to a woman whose faithfulness to her husband was in question. If she were an adulterous wife, the bitter water would go into her belly and bring a curse.

A closer look at this story brings an interesting application for us. The word for *belly* that is found in Numbers 5 can by extension mean *heart*.[4] When we swallow the bitter things of this life and allow them to remain in our hearts, the curse begins to operate against us. God doesn't want us to be cursed, though. He wants us to be blessed! The progression of this curse in the belly or heart doesn't stop there. *"And this water that causeth the curse shall go into thy bowels, to make thy belly to swell, and thy thigh to rot…"* (Numbers 5:22). The word for *bowels* is also figuratively the word for *emotions*.[5] Bitterness affects our hearts, our emotions, and will eventually affect even our bodies.

"And the priest shall write these curses in a book, and he shall blot them out with the bitter water; And he shall cause the woman to drink the bitter water that causeth the curse; and the water that causeth the curse shall enter into her and become bitter" (Numbers 5: 23,24). The Bible goes on to say that her belly would swell and her thigh would rot. Have you ever heard a sermon on the Swollen Belly or the Rotten Thigh? I doubt it. This is not a popular topic.

These curses that the priest used have already been written out for us. They are found in Deuteronomy 28. Oh yes, the first fourteen verses contain wonderful promises of blessings: blessed in the city, blessed in the country, blessed coming in and going out. We love these blessings. Many of us probably have those verses underlined. But have you noticed there are 14 verses on the blessings and 53 verses on the curses? You probably haven't underlined the curses, but they're still a part of God's Word.

The entire key to Deuteronomy 28 is to understand obedience and disobedience. When we walk in obedience to God's Word, we are under the blessings; but if we become disobedient, we have opened ourselves up to the curses. Please understand in the story of the bitter waters that the word *curse* means the removal of a rightful and blessed state. When we don't deal with the bitter waters in our hearts, then we are in disobedience to the God who tells us to put away all bitterness. *"Let all bitterness, and wrath, and anger, and clamour, and evil speaking, be put away from you, with all malice: And be kind one to another, tenderhearted, forgiving one another, even as God for Christ's sake hath forgiven you"* (Ephesians 4:31,32).

When we don't put away our bitterness but instead cling to it, we may be in danger of the curse found in Deuteronomy 28:60-61. *"Moreover he will bring upon thee all the diseases of Egypt, which thou was afraid of; and they shall cleave unto thee. Also every sickness, and every plague, which is not written in the book of this law, them will the LORD bring upon thee, until thou be destroyed."* This sounds almost identical to the word in Exodus 15:26. *"If you will diligently hearken to the voice of the LORD thy God, and will do that which is right in his sight, and will give ear to his commandments and keep his statutes, I will put none of these diseases upon thee, which I have brought upon the Egyptians; for I am the Lord that healeth thee."*

Please realize that if we don't find a way to heal our Marahs, through the bitter waters we have swallowed our emotions will swell. That may seem like an odd thought, but have you ever overreacted to a situation and then wondered why? I have become aware that when I "lose it" emotionally for what seems to be no reason, I'd better run a self-check for bitterness. In a manner of speaking, at times I have accepted bitter water in my belly and heart, and if left unchecked this water opens the door for disease to enter.

Our Healer; Our Redeemer

God has provided healing for us. Don't forget His promise at the Pool of Marah. He is our physician and can heal us on every level—physical, mental, emotional, and spiritual. Remember the cure we saw in Chapter One? We need to put a tree in the bitter water—the tree of Calvary for our health and healing—by bringing all these needs and concerns to Jesus, the One who can transform our lives. Isaiah 53 says this:

"Surely he hath borne our griefs, and carried our sorrows: yet we did esteem him stricken, smitten of God, and afflicted. But he was wounded for our transgressions, he was bruised for our iniquities: the chastise-

ment of our peace was upon him; and with his stripes we are healed. All we like sheep have gone astray; we have turned every one to his own way; and the LORD hath laid on him the iniquity of us all" (verses 4-6).

Jesus not only took our sins upon Himself, He was bruised that we would have peace. Do we want to lose that peace because of bitterness? It's a simple equation: once we let bitterness in, it seems as if our peace goes out. Bitterness in=peace out. Jesus wants to be our Prince of Peace; and if we can apply the tree of Calvary to all of our Marahs, we can receive healing in any area of our lives where the curse is trying to operate against us.

"Christ has redeemed us from the curse of the law, being made a curse for us; for it is written, Cursed is every one that hangeth on a tree" (Galatians 3:13). We have been redeemed from the curse of the law, but not yet from the curse of the fall. As soon as Adam and Eve sinned in the garden, mankind came under the curse of the fall. God spoke to Adam regarding his sin, and in his bitterness Adam said, "It's the woman you gave me." Can you see him shifting the blame from himself to Eve and also to God? The woman YOU gave me. Let's not forget that when Eve was being tempted by the serpent, Adam was by her side. *"And when the woman saw that the tree was good for food and that it was pleasant to the eyes, and a tree to be desired to make one wise, she took of the fruit thereof, and did eat, and gave also <u>unto her husband with her; and he did eat</u>"* (Genesis 3:6, emphasis added). When Eve was confronted by the Lord, she was bitter: *"The serpent beguiled me and I did eat."* Believe it or not, we make very similar excuses, not taking responsibility for our own actions.

There were two trees in the garden: the tree of life and the tree of the knowledge of good and evil. The tree of life was not forbidden to Adam and Eve until they disobeyed by eating the fruit from the tree of the knowledge of good and evil. If, after sinning, Adam had eaten of the tree of life, he would have continued in sin and disobedience. To prevent this, Adam was escorted out of the Garden of Eden. God then installed His plan for the redemption of man, determining that there would have to be another tree, a second Adam, and another garden.

"And so it is written, the first man Adam was made a living soul, the last Adam was made a quickening spirit. Howbeit that was not first which is spiritual but that which is natural; and afterward that which is spiritual. The first man is of earth, earthy; the second man is the Lord from heaven." (1 Corinthians 15:45-47). We can see from this passage that Jesus came as the second or final Adam. The garden he went to wasn't Eden but Gethsemane.

In His garden, Jesus accepted the cup of suffering. Thank God! Through His obedience, atonement was made for the Fall and the sins of mankind. When Jesus died on the tree, it was to redeem us from the curse of disobedience—the curse bringing sickness and death. Because of what He has done, we can join David in saying, *"Bless the Lord, O my soul, and all that is within me bless his holy name. Bless the Lord, O my soul, and forget not all his benefits: Who forgiveth all thine iniquities; who healeth all thy diseases"* (Psalm 103:1-3).

We have atonement because of the tree of Calvary, and by the blood of Jesus we have forgiveness and deliverance. We can take our bitter waters to Him, and He will give us living waters.

How About You?

1. Do you feel as though you are experiencing a dry time in your Christian walk? Are you reading the Word daily for a fresh infilling? Praying and staying in prayer until you sense His presence? Confessing each day's sins and receiving forgiveness?

2. Do you still have any pools of Mara that need to be made sweet? What are they?

3. How can you reverse the curse that comes after you have swallowed a bitter pill?

4. What has Jesus done for you personally? Take a moment and pray through Psalm 23, meditating on the promises and blessings of God.

Endnotes

1. Definition taken from *Strong's Exhaustive Concordance*

2. *Ibid.*

3. *Handbook on the Pentateuch*, Victor P. Hamilton

4. Definitions for words in this paragraph come from The Complete Word Study Old Testament, Zodhiates, AMG Publishers

Symptoms

We're going to examine bitterness from a little different angle in this chapter. There are definite symptoms that mark bitterness of spirit. Our attitude should always be that of King David: *"Search me, O God, and know my heart: try me, and know my thoughts: And see if there be any wicked way in me, and lead me in the way everlasting"* (Psalm 139:23,24). We don't want to harbor bitterness—even unconsciously—and we'll soon discover that the words that come out of our mouths can be a real indicator of what is actually in our hearts. A key Bible character who can illustrate this next topic is a gentleman named Job.

Job was a very powerful and influential man from the Middle East. In fact, if Job had lived in modern times he would undoubtedly be published in *Forbes*, as well as being listed in the *Fortune 500*. His picture would be plastered on billboards and on the cover of *Newsweek*, and he'd have a regular column in *Entrepreneur*.

Several millennia ago, Job was the wealthiest man in the Middle East.

The extent of his wealth is published in the Old Testament, where an entire book was written about him and even bears his name. The Bible tells us that Job lived in the land of Uz; checking *Strong's Concordance* we find that *Uz* means, "to take advice or counsel together." It also means "firmness."[1] I am sure that Job gave great counsel and could, at times, be very firm. Have you ever been around the rich and famous? They can be extremely firm and yet they have their chosen counselors, too. The rich are also hounded by others for advice.

Not only did Job live in Uz, we also know this about him: he *"was perfect and upright, and one that feared God, and eschewed evil"* (Job 1:1b). Probably all of us would like to know how to make money and influence people, but if the only way to do it is to be perfect, that's another story. *Strong's Concordance* includes these synonyms under the Hebrew word that we have translated perfect: pious, gentle, plain, undefiled, and upright. The Lexical Aids to the Old Testament in the Hebrew-Greek Key Study Bible gives the definitions "sincere, a person of integrity." Job was a man to be respected and admired for spiritual qualities as well.

We also know of Job that he fathered a large family: ten children. Of course, with his money he could have as many children as he wanted. I doubt that in his day sandals sold for the price of a pair of Nikes, Reeboks, or Fila sneakers. I remember one occasion, just a few years ago, when my son, Matthew, wanted to purchase a new pair of sneakers at our local mall. Being a generous mother, and totally out of touch with what things cost at the end of the nineties, I gave him $30. Believe it or not, I expected some change, too. My son just started to laugh. It seems the sneakers he wanted were almost $100 per pair. Whatever happened to the *bobo* sneakers I could purchase for $19.99—in different colors no less?

A Challenge in the Heavens

Keeping what we know of Job in mind, that he was perfect, fearing God and avoiding evil; he was a sincere man of integrity; he was blessed with family and riches; let's consider what he lacked. Job had no ability to see into the heavens, no insight into spiritual realms. While all seemed peaceful on earth and Job's children had gathered for a birthday party, Job was offering sacrifices for his children in the event that one or more of them might have sinned in some way or *"cursed God in their hearts. Thus Job did continually"* (Job 1:5*b*). At the same time, Job was unaware of a challenge taking place in heaven. This challenge concerned Job and his entire family.

"Now there was a day when the sons of God came to present themselves before the Lord, and Satan came also among them...And the Lord said unto Satan, Hast thou considered my servant Job, that there is none like him in the earth, a perfect and an upright man, one that feareth God, and escheweth evil?" (Job 1:6,8). It really blessed me to notice that the Lord was proud of Job because Job served God. He wasn't proud of him because he was rich or well known, or because he was powerful or had family status. The important thing was that he was a servant of God.

Satan responded that the only reason Job was a servant of God was that God had given him all the pleasures of life. In essence, the devil was saying that Job was only serving God "for what he could get." That doesn't sound like a man of integrity to me. Satan then wanted God to "touch" all that Job had, feeling sure that then Job would curse God.

The Lord reminded Satan that all that Job had here on earth was in his power, however there was one important stipulation: Satan wasn't allowed to kill Job. Now comes the part of Job's life we are most familiar with—his time of misery and bitterness of heart.

"And there was a day when his sons and his daughters were eating and drinking wine in their eldest brother's house: And there came a messenger unto Job, and said, "The oxen were plowing, and the asses feeding beside them: And the Sabeans fell upon them, and took them away; yea they have slain the servants with the edge of the sword; and I only am escaped alone to tell thee" (Job 1:13-15).

Immediately afterwards, this same sort of message was delivered to him regarding his sheep, his camels, his servants, and *all* of his children. All were attacked, burned, crushed, or slain. What a terribly series of tragedies! Job was devastated and yet he still worshipped God. Seeing this, Satan told God that he figured Job would change his tune if Job experienced physical suffering himself. *"But put forth thine hand now, and touch his bone and his flesh, and he will curse thee to thy face"* (Job 2:5)

God had more faith in Job than that, and allowed Satan to try this test. *"So went Satan forth from the presence of the Lord, and smote Job with sore boils from the sole of his foot unto his crown. And he took him a potsherd to scrape himself withal; and he sat down among the ashes"* (Job 2:7,8).

Job was hit in four areas of his life that affect all of us: his finances, family, friends, and his flesh. It seems the only thing that the enemy left Job was his wife. As a woman, I am sorry to say that many times the enemy will use us against our nearest and dearest. *"Then said his wife unto him, Dost thou still retain thine integrity? Curse God, and die"* (Job 2:9). She obviously didn't have the spiritual insight to realize this was a test and trial of Job's faith and his allegiance to God. I doubt she even realized that she was serving as a mouthpiece for Satan. Had Job been influenced by her at this point, Satan would have accomplished his mission against the man of God.

The Integrity Question

Proverbs 31 has a great deal to say about the role of a woman, particularly the role of a wife. How should Job's wife have spoken to him in this time of great affliction? *"She openeth her mouth with wisdom and in her tongue is the law of kindness"* (Proverbs 31:26). I don't think we have a match here. She wasn't using wisdom, nor were her words kind. When people are suffering or undergoing times of trial, we need to weigh our words very carefully. Sometimes less is better. We certainly don't want to be used by the enemy to bring bitterness.

Job, the great man of integrity, remained faithful in spite of his wife's advice. After the terrible heartache of losing his children, his wealth, and then even his health, he did not sin against God. Even when his wife challenged his relationship with God, asking him *"Dost thou still retain thy integrity?"* (Job 2:9), Job did not sin.

What kind of a question is that for a wife to ask her husband anyway. We know what Job thought. He said, *"Thou speakest as one of the foolish women speaketh. What? shall we receive good at the hand of God, and shall we not receive evil?"* (Job 2:10*a*). He really hit the nail on the head. She was speaking as a foolish woman. What woman would want her husband to be without integrity? In all of this the Word says Job did not sin with his lips. I can't say the same for his wife.

Under such pressure as this, would we be able to retain our integrity? Would we share Job's philosophy that naked he came out of his mother's womb, and naked he would go to his tomb? He still blessed and worshipped the Lord in the midst of his tragedy. What an inspiration for us!

The next event in Job's life was the arrival of some of his friends who came to comfort him. When they saw his grief and pain, they lifted up their voices and began to weep for him. The Bible says Job's grief was so great that his friends couldn't even speak.

Finally, Job begins to talk to his friends. Notice that he still doesn't curse God, although his bitterness of heart is evident: *"let the day perish wherin I was born, and the night in which it was said, There is a man child conceived...Let them curse it that curse the day, who are ready to raise up their mourning"* (Job 3:3,8). In essence, Job says he wishes he had never been born. Please remember that after Satan left the presence of God, he had all of Job's children killed in a terrible accident, raiders came and took away much of his livestock, and the rest of the stock was destroyed in freak accidents. Job lost his family and his wealth in a moment's time and then was covered with boils from crown to foot, all courtesy the devil—although Job didn't know that. In his condition, who *wouldn't* say, "I wish I had never been born"?

Have you ever had any trouble with your children, or have you ever

45

heard a teenager say, "I didn't ask to be born?" I remember many years ago when my daughter was very young and very unhappy about some decision I had made, she said to me, "I never asked to be born!" My answer to her was this, "If you had asked, the answer would have been NO!" Of course I didn't mean that, but it certainly ended our little debate, and not on the best note, either. There can be times in our lives when we temporarily feel sorry that we've been born, but Job's problems may be unparalleled throughout history. I believe he really meant what he said.

Emerging Symptoms

"The heart knoweth his own bitterness" (Proverbs 14:10*a*). Since bitterness is of the heart, how do we know that Job began to experience bitterness? We can't see into someone's heart, but certain symptoms indicate that bitterness is there. Jesus said, *"...out of the abundance of the heart, the mouth speaketh"* (Matthew 12:34). When anyone has bitterness in his heart— whether Job, you, or I—it will eventually come out of the mouth. How careful we must be to watch what we are saying and not get into the habit of speaking negative things! The things we say can bring us down and discourage those around us, too.

Another area affected by bitterness is the soul. *"Wherefore is light given to him that is in misery and life unto the bitter of soul"* (Job 3:20). You are a spirit, you live in a body, and you have a soul. This is confirmed in the New Testament: *"And I pray God your whole spirit and soul and body be preserved blameless unto the coming of our Lord Jesus Christ"* (1 Thessalonians 5:23). Job's bitterness was in his *soul* because the soul is the realm of our feelings, thoughts, and emotions. Some would say that the soul consists of the mind, the will, and the emotions.

Although bitterness is a matter of the heart, it deeply affects our soulish being. Just take a look at Job. He claimed he was in misery, and both with his mind and his emotions he was experiencing and expressing bitterness. *"My soul is weary of my life, I will leave my complaint upon myself; I will speak in the bitterness of my soul"* (Job 10:1). Moving from the King James

46

to the modern translations, we find the Amplified Bible renders this *"I will give free expression to my complaint,"* the New International Version says, *"I will give free rein to my complaint,"* and the New American Standard says, *"I will give full vent to my complaint."*

As Job did indeed speak in the bitterness of his soul, we see several symptoms in this one verse. He is fed up with life and he continually complains—especially about himself. One way to diagnose bitterness is to listen to the words of those around you, but also listen to your own words. If you have been affected by bitterness and allow yourself to complain, you usually sound something like this, "You don't know what they did to <u>me</u>, or how much <u>I</u> have suffered. Why did the Lord do this to <u>me</u>? <u>I</u> am so hurt. <u>I</u> have been sinned against. <u>My</u> suffering is so unbearable." And on and on it goes.

Have you ever been around someone who, no matter what good things happen, still finds a way to remain negative? You know the deal: the glass is always half empty and never half full. People who are bitter seem to go through life with a weary and disgusted outlook. I know this doesn't pertain to you, dear reader, but surely you know someone who suffers from this negative mind-set. Not very attractive, is it? People affected by bitterness have a whole catalog of complaints, but they sound like a broken record. Round and round, over and over again, they recite their woes— never being aware of what is happening in their own heart and soul.

Several years ago, I actually lived this verse of Job's in my personal life, *"giving free expression to my complaint."* I was not just a hearer of the Word, but a doer—at least of this particular verse. I can't go into the detail I would like to about the problems I went through, but I can tell you that Satan hit me over and over again. I cried every day for almost a month. Talk about a complainer, I had my sufferings listed in alphabetical order. I talked non-stop about the injustice that had been done to me, asking why God had put this on me, etc., etc.,…round and round. See any symptoms? And did you notice the error in my reasoning? I actually thought God had put my problems on me. Job made the same mistake.

He began to blame God for what was really an attack of the enemy. Job wallowed in the bitterness of his soul. Many times we do, too. When the enemy attacks, we often accuse God.

I learned that the hardest thing for the believer on any given day is to discern whether something is a correction from the Lord or abuse from Satan. Often we are so busy trying to submit to God that we fail to resist the enemy. At other times, we keep rebuking spirits and pleading the blood over the very correction that will preserve our lives.

When we are bitter, we are angry, touchy, or testy. We may try to blame our bitterness on PMS (Permanent Mental Stress, my definition), but the truth is that for some reason or another, we have taken offense. When you see some of these symptoms in yourself, quickly go to the Lord and ask Him to reveal what you are bitter about. It took me a long time to get relief from the problems I experienced, and I believe that my deliverance was delayed because of the words of my mouth. Like Job, I gave free rein to my complaints; and the more my soul spoke, the more weary and miserable I became.

Let's look a little deeper into Job's experience. *"Therefore I will not refrain my mouth, I will speak in the anguish of my spirit, I will complain in the bitterness of my soul"* (Job 7:11). Do you see the symptoms we've talked about? Once again we have the open mouth, complaining with no restraint, and bitterness of soul; however something new has been added: anguish of spirit.

Bitterness can easily move from the area of our soul to the area of our spirit. I believe when bitterness reaches into our spirit, some real roots begin to grow. Unfortunately, by their very nature, roots are underground and therefore more difficult to detect. Job's anguish of spirit represented an increase in bitterness. By the time I reached this stage, I no longer thought I was "letting off steam" by voicing my complaints. There was no relief for me in unloading my troubles to someone else. I was becoming someone who was unable to speak anything but negative comments and

Chapter 3   Symptoms

bitter thoughts.

What exactly is anguish of spirit? Try "intense inner turmoil." When bitter roots have begun to grow, we will experience a great deal of inner turmoil. Sometimes that brings the sort of confusion where we can't really define what we're feeling, but we know that there is a problem deep inside us.

Let's back up, for a moment, to the word *complain*, as Job used it. Most of us feel certain we could give an accurate definition of the word complain. How about "to express grief, pain, or discontent; to make a formal accusation or charge"? That's what Webster's dictionary says; however, there is a much more powerful definition to this common word. Before I give you this definition, allow me to share a personal testimony regarding a Holy Spirit revelation during a time when I had been giving free rein to all the complaining my soul and my spirit could muster.

When Division Enters

In the late 1970s, my husband and I purchased a home in a very small development. We were really hungry for Christian fellowship, and with less than a dozen homes in our neighborhood, the chances of having Christian neighbors seemed pretty slim. We prayed to God that we would find someone of like faith nearby. The more we thought about it and talked together, we felt perhaps we should pray for the opportunity to lead someone to Christ. Then not only would we have fellowship, but we could also disciple a new believer.

Shortly after this decision, a new house was built right behind our home. As the foundation of the house was poured, I was reading the story of Joshua. You remember—God told Joshua to march around Jericho seven times and the walls of that city would fall down. I told my husband, Concepcion—or "Boo" for short—that I wanted to pray and march around this new foundation in order to claim for Christ whoever bought the house. Boo said we'd better march before the walls were erected or they just might fall down! We were new Christians at the time, and we took God at His word, plain and simple. I laugh now at the simplicity of our childlike faith; however, childlike or not, I had too much pride to march in the daylight. I told Boo we should wait until it got dark. Then we'd apply our faith, march around the slab of concrete, and believe God to send us someone whose heart was prepared to receive Jesus.

We went out in the dark like some kind of secret agents—undercover for the Lord. I remember it was raining, but we still marched around and around until we were both dizzy. (You can read the directions for yourself in Joshua chapter 6.) God told Joshua to march for seven days. The first six days they only went around the city once. Then on the seventh day they were to hold their peace while marching around the city seven times, and then they were to give a mighty shout. We condensed this to just one night, since we didn't want to be seen, and we marched fast!

If someone armed with a video camera had been in the woods across the street, I feel certain they could have won considerable cash by sending a tape of us to America's Funniest Home Videos. Here were two so-called adults, silently circling a foundation twelve times; then on the thirteenth time they shout, race inside their own house, and quickly close the drapes.

It wasn't long, though, until the house was finished and a nice young family moved in. Our new neighbors had one little girl and another child on the way. I wanted to welcome them to the development, but I'm not the Dolly Domestic type who wears an apron and hands a homemade cake across the white picket fence to the new neighbors. For one thing, I don't bake. So "Sara Lee" and I made a little visit next door. As our friendship grew, so did my new neighbor's stomach. In just a few weeks after moving into their new home, they welcomed an addition to their family—another beautiful baby girl.

One evening Boo was able to share his faith with his new friend next door, and this gentleman opened his heart to the Lord. Right there in our family room, the two men prayed together and he was wonderfully saved.

He asked us not to tell his wife, and we agreed—sure that this was something he wanted to share with her personally. When he left our house that evening, we were rejoicing at the privilege of leading someone to Christ. We were so excited that we couldn't fall asleep. Consequently, we were still awake when his van started up. We wondered where he would be going that late at night.

Finally, we both fell asleep, only to be awakened in the middle of the night by a State Trooper knocking on our door. Our new neighbor, and now our new brother in the Lord, had been in a terrible car accident. The State Trooper asked if one of us could go over and stay with the children while he took the wife to the hospital. Boo offered to sit with the children so that I could go to the hospital as well and keep our neighbor's wife company.

At the hospital, we were told the grim news that our neighbor probably wouldn't live through the night. Evidently, he had been driving to a local convenience store, fell asleep at the wheel, and hit a telephone pole head-on. Since his van was the style with the engine in the back instead of the front, there was nothing to cushion the impact. His injuries were terribly severe.

I didn't want to break my promise to him; but with his life hanging by a thread, I felt that his wife needed to know about his eternal status. I told her that he had just received the gift of salvation by praying the sinner's prayer at our home hours earlier. She then wanted to know what she needed to do to be saved. I shared the gospel with her, and Christ came into her heart and life.

How she would need Him in the weeks and months ahead! Her husband didn't die, but the road to recovery was very long and hard for both of them. Also during this time, as he was in and out of the hospital and had several surgeries, Boo and I developed a very close friendship with them. They began attending the same church we did, and eventually we even had Bible studies in their home. Our children all became very good

51

friends, and for almost ten years, the four of us adults were inseparable—praying and playing together.

It's hard to be that close without experiencing some disagreements, and at times we experienced tension in our relationship. For a long time, we were able to work out the difficulties and resume wonderful Christian fellowship. In fact, we felt we were truly family as well as friends. But one night all of that changed. We returned home from another couple's house and were amazed to find several articles on our front porch—all items of ours that they had borrowed or used with our permission.

We were baffled. What had happened? Why would they want to return our possessions without talking to us? Naturally, we went to their home, but they didn't want to discuss the problem or restore the relationship. We made several attempts to resolve the situation, but to no avail. It was very hard and painful for all of us to see each other, attend the same church, and have no real fellowship or communication.

Time went by. I began to harden my heart since I couldn't correct the problem. After all, I didn't even know what the problem was! I moved on with my life and with new friendships, all the time thinking I didn't have any unforgiveness or bitterness because this was *their* problem. I was just trying to survive the rejection.

Then my daughter, Mimi, who was about to be married, asked if we could invite their family to the wedding. I couldn't very well object, seeing that our children had been so close. I knew she wanted their entire family to enjoy her special day, but at the wedding I still sensed the tension and ongoing rejection.

I was disturbed for a long time following the wedding whenever I would think of them and the past, but God used this event in my life to show me that I had great bitterness against them.

A Silent Symptom

Now we come back to the extra definition for *complain* that I said I would tell you. This word for complain doesn't have anything to do with verbal expression. Surprise! I always thought complaining was speaking in a negative way to register displeasure. But the definition of the Hebrew word for complain also has to do with rehearsing a matter over and over again. This is a rehearsal in the mind. For my part, I realized that even though our friendship had been dissolved years ago, I was still rehearsing the events over and over in my mind. The Lord even told me that I was having dress rehearsals!

Does any of this sound familiar? Can you relate to thoughts such as "I should have said this or that," or "If only I had done thus and so," or "The next time I see them I'll say…" Doesn't the word rehearse mean to practice and repeat and drill something until you know it by heart? Believe me, I have done so; and I suspect that at some point in your life, you may have done this, too.

Once I understood this definition of *complain,* I had to admit to myself and to God that I was indeed complaining due to the bitterness of my soul. Not being verbal, this symptom will not be immediately evident to others; but we need to police our own thoughts, being careful not to dwell on areas that don't draw us closer to Christ. The Word says we are to be *"Casting down imaginations, and every high thing that exalteth itself against the knowledge of God, and bringing into captivity every thought to the obedience of Christ"* (2 Corinthians 10:4). We are also instructed to be renewed: *"And be not conformed to this world: but be ye transformed by the renewing of your mind, that ye may prove what is that good, and acceptable, and perfect, will of God"* (Romans 12:2). Finally, we are to focus on the positive and the good: *"…whatsoever things are true, whatsoever things are pure, whatsoever things are lovely, whatsoever things are of good report; if there be any virtue, and if there be any praise, think on these things"* (Philippians 4:8).

You might want to pause for a moment here and ask the Holy Spirit to help you identify frequent thoughts that need to be brought captive to Christ. He who has promised is faithful to cleanse us from all unrighteousness—but we must confess and ask His forgiveness.

I had to repent of my bitterness over the broken friendship, and I had to ask God for forgiveness. Aren't you glad that we have a God who forgives completely? I felt led to pray that there would be healing for my life as well as the lives of my neighbors and former friends.

You need to know that this was not a one-time prayer, though. I had prayed blessings in the area of relationships for several months when I was asked to speak at a women's retreat. I knew that the church involved was the church my estranged neighbor attended. I accepted the invitation to speak, fully expecting that when she found out I was the speaker, she wouldn't come to the retreat. How thankful I am that she did attend! My first sermon was on the healing of the bitter waters, but my neighbor and I did not experience immediate restoration at that service. In the morning, however, there was a great breakthrough. After years of broken fellowship, we fell into each others' arms, both of us crying streams of tears. Truly the tree of Calvary was able to turn the bitter waters to sweet ones. I am so grateful for the Lord's provision!

Bitterness Revealed through Other Symptoms

There are some other symptoms of bitterness that we need to examine. Poor Job is the source for several of them. In fact, an entire series of symptoms comes from Job 23:1-9, and the first one may come as a surprise. *"Even today is my complaint rebellious and bitter"* (Job 23:2*a*, Amplified Bible). Rebellion is a very serious sin. As a matter of fact, the Bible tells us *"For rebellion is as the sin of witchcraft"* (1 Samuel 15:23*a*). Think about this. We know we are to have nothing to do with witchcraft of any kind, and yet when we allow bitterness into our hearts, we are being rebellious.

"Oh that I knew where I might find him! That I might come even to his seat! I would order my cause before him, and fill my mouth with arguments"

(Job 23:3). With the bitterness in his heart, Job is rebellious and he cannot find God. He then says that if he knew where to find God, he would fill his mouth with arguments. Have you observed this, too? When people are bitter to the point of rebelliousness, they want to argue all the time. Often it seems futile to try to reason with them because, until the Lord shows them their bitterness of heart, they are only looking for a fight.

Job wanted to argue to the point of having a "dispute" with the Lord (v. 7). Can you imagine wanting to argue or dispute with God? Job was still in the self-defense mode. Ah, now that's something we might admit to. Most of us have had moments, at least, of wanting to justify ourselves in the eyes of others, to defend our own behavior. We need to check our *real* motives when we find ourselves getting defensive.

"Behold, I go forward, but he is not there; and backward, but I cannot perceive him" (Job 23:8). In my life this has been one of the worst fruits from a bitter tree. I can sing, pray, attend church, read my Bible, and still not perceive the presence of the Lord. I don't believe the Lord hides Himself, as Job accuses Him of doing. I do believe that the bitterness in our hearts separates us from Him.

One of the most important things we need to remember when we read the book of Job is that Job said many things while in a state of confusion. *"If I be wicked, woe unto me; and if I be righteous, yet will I not lift up my head. I am full of confusion"* (Job 10:15). Consider what it means to be confused. When we are confused, we are mixed-up mentally, and therefore, we can't distinguish between the truth and a lie. Job illustrated this in that he couldn't distinguish between the hand of God and the hand of the enemy. Notice that when God answered Job out of the whirlwind, He said, *"Who is this that darkeneth counsel by words without knowledge?"* (Job 38:2).

The Whole Truth and Nothing But the Truth...

Let's be careful to quote our verses in context. The Bible is definitely the infallible Word of God. Men of God wrote the sacred Scriptures as they were moved by the Holy Spirit. (See 2 Peter 1:20,21.) We need to understand that although the Bible was written under that inspiration, not everything written is inspired. Please let me explain. When the Bible was written, it recorded not only the words of God, but also the words of men, the statements of the devil, and even some conversations with angels. We know that the Bible is true and truly written; however, can you see that not everything that has been truly written is true? I'll explain further.

We know that Satan is a liar. Jesus calls him the *"father of lies and of all that is false"* (John 8:44*b*, Amplified Bible). Several times, the words of Satan are recorded in the Bible when he is having conversations with Jesus or Adam and Eve. We'd better be sure we have no confusion about who is speaking when we read the Word. Ask who is speaking. Is it God, or man, or even Satan? If it's not God, then we may have to ask if what is being said is a true statement. After all, God's rebuke to Job, that Job was speaking words without knowledge, shows us we'd better be careful how we quote the book of Job. During Job's time of confusion, what he said was certainly not reliable—according to the best possible authority: God. When Job finally was drawn out of his confusion, he had enough sense to put his hand over his mouth.

Once I understood this principle, it was easier to understand some of the statements in the book of Job, as well as other scriptures. Job said, *"...the arrows of the Almighty are within me"* (Job 6:4*a*). Yes, it's true that Job said this, but what Job said was not true. Job didn't have the insight to realize that God wasn't the one afflicting him.

After the Lord spoke to Job (Job 38-41), we see a change in Job's attitude as reflected through the words of his mouth. Job doesn't argue or dispute with God. He repents with his hand over his mouth. Because of this, he is about to recover all he had lost. The same can be true for us when we repent of our bitterness. Rather than being a continual rehearsal of painful incidents, our conversation will express delight and joy in God's grace and salvation.

How About You?

1. Are you able to see any of these symptoms in your life? How about in the life of a loved one?

2. Have there been times when you were bitter at God, only to find out that God didn't afflict you?

3. What will you do with the memory of bitter events in your life?

4. Have you ever suffered the loss of a close friendship? What strategy should you use to heal this relationship? Will the reconciliation happen immediately?

5. Keep track of what you say and how you say it (tone of voice) to family and friends for one day. If you hear yourself making negative statements, ask the Lord to show you why. Then, ask for His grace in becoming an encouragement to others.

End Notes

1. *The Exhaustive Dictionary of Bible Names* by Dr. Judson Cornwall and Dr. Stelman Smith.

Chapter 4

The Gall of It All

One of the sneakiest and nastiest things about bitterness is that we can get to the point where we are enjoying our own misery. Talk about a paradox, and yet isn't it so? We actually make a choice to remain bitter. Don't forget that old saying, either: "Misery loves company."

The Scriptures have much to say about bitterness, but there are some other key words that often appear with bitterness. (As I said—misery loves company.) Two words that are associated in the Bible with bitterness are *gall* and *wormwood*. One such reference occurs as a warning in the Old Testament. *"Lest there should be among you man, or woman, or family, or tribe, whose heart turneth away this day from the LORD our God, to go and serve the gods of these nations; lest there should be among you a root that beareth gall and wormwood"* (Deuteronomy 29:18). I find it interesting that the first time in the Old Testament that we are introduced to the word *wormwood*, the verse also speaks about a root that bears gall. Probably the most familiar verse in the Bible dealing with bitterness is in the context of a New Testament warning: *"Follow peace with all men, and holiness, without which no man shall see the* LORD; *Looking diligently lest any man fail of the grace of God; lest any root of bitterness springing up trouble you and thereby many be defiled"* (Hebrews 12:14,15). It's the root of gall and the root of bitterness that put us in danger of the curse.

There are other references which tie wormwood to bitterness. *"And the name of the star is called Wormwood; and the third part of the waters became wormwood; and many men died of the waters, because they were made bitter"* (Revelation 8:11). Isn't it interesting that the waters became bitter and were called wormwood? There's another scripture in the book of Jeremiah that correlates wormwood with water and gall. *"Therefore thus saith the Lord of hosts, the God of Israel; Behold, I will feed them, even this people, with wormwood, and give them water of gall to drink"* (Jeremiah 9:15). And again, *"Behold I will feed them with wormwood, and make them to drink the water of gall"* (Jeremiah 23:15).

We're getting the idea that wormwood is not a good thing, and that it is connected with bitterness, but what exactly is it? *Strong's Exhaustive Concordance* reveals that in the Old Testament, the word *wormwood* means "to curse, something regarded as poisonous." In the New Testament, the word translated *wormwood* also refers to "a type of bitterness or calamity." The prophet Jeremiah certainly went through many different calamities in his life and ministry; and at one point in his life, he was full of bitterness. As we look at this prophet, we will get an idea of the damage that wormwood and gall can do in our personal lives.

Remembering Our Affliction and Misery

In the book of Lamentations, Jeremiah expresses what occurred when the poison of gall set into him. *"He hath filled me with bitterness, he hath made me drunken with the wormwood. He hath also broken my teeth with gravel stones, he hath covered me with ashes. And thou hast removed my soul far off from peace; I forgot prosperity. And I said My strength and my hope is perished from the* LORD. *Remembering mine affliction and my misery, the wormwood and the gall"* (Lamentations 3:15-19). The prophet was obviously under a curse. He centered on his misery and the bad treatment he had received. Oh the gall of it all!

"Remembering mine affliction and my misery, the wormwood and the gall..." Isn't his language vivid? We feel his pain in what the prophet declares. As I have sought the Lord for healing for the bitterness in my own life, I have become very sure of one principle. When things happen that cause us to get bitter—or if we have been wounded, hurt, or offended, and these pains are not dealt with—we not only remember our affliction, bad treatment, and misery, but as we remember them we also *relive* the incidents that cause them. Be sure you notice the word I used is relive and not relieve. We tend to think we'll find relief or some sort of answer by reliving the hurtful episode, but the very opposite is true.

A bitter spirit has an acute memory, but that memory may be riddled with irrational distortions. I am not happy about this pattern in my own life. I can quickly recall things from my childhood that hurt me. Not only can I recall them, but also the details seem to be indelibly etched on my mind. (Is the same true for you? Be honest.) However, a few years ago, I would still have argued with you that my early home life was a healthy one. I remembered the hurtful things that directly affected me, yet I denied that as a family we had any problems.

I first became aware of this destructive pattern several years ago when my older brother and I had dinner together. He lived in Florida then, and I took him out to dinner to celebrate his birthday and just to spend some time with him. During the meal, we shared some of our favorite stories from our childhood.

To my utter amazement, we had two totally different interpretations of the same events—in fact, the memories of much of our early home life didn't line up at all. My brother opened up to me about how disturbing and disquieting our childhood had been. Even now as an adult, some of those things still affected him. For my part, this sounded so foreign. Where had I been when all of this was taking place? My brother is five years older than I am, but from our different perspectives, you would have thought we grew up in different cities and were raised by different parents.

When I returned home from the visit with my older brother, I had some real soul-searching to do. I needed to face the truth and admit that I had experienced some serious problems in my childhood. Years ago we didn't have all the television talk shows which discuss how children from dysfunctional homes are handicapped—or even simply what a dysfunctional home is. But I'm here to tell you that dysfunctional homes are not something new. The first dysfunctional home is found in the Garden of Eden. After Adam and Eve sinned, the husband and wife blamed each other for the problems they had. Their troubles didn't end there, either. Look at their first two children. Many people believe Cain and Abel were twins because the Word only comments on her conceiving once before she bore the two sons.

Trouble was probably already there, but we first read about relational problems in the account of the two brothers bringing their offerings before the Lord. The Bible states it bluntly: *"And Cain talked with Abel his brother: and it came to pass, when they were in the field, that Cain rose up against Abel his brother, and slew him"* (Genesis 4:8). Murder in the first degree—and in the very first family. Cain was then driven out from his home and family. Think of Eve's heartbreak! She lost both her sons, one to murder and one to banishment. Let's face it, dysfunction has been with us for centuries. (See Genesis 3-4.)

Before I share some of the gall and bitterness from my childhood, I want to give hope to all parents and provide some relief for the hidden guilt that may lurk in many of our hearts. I have made many mistakes as a mother and a parent—just like my parents and grandparents before me. After all, my parenting skills were developed from observation of my parents. They, in turn, were taught by their parents.

The enemy is an expert at bringing up our past failures and mistakes. There isn't anything we can do to change the past, and his torment does not allow us to move on with our lives and recover from our past. The

Bible actually teaches us to forget the former things. *"Brethren, I count not myself to have apprehended: but this one thing I do, forgetting those things which are behind, and reaching forth unto those things which are before, I press toward the mark for the prize of the high calling of God in Christ Jesus,"* (Philippians 3:13-14). Notice that Paul says, "this one thing I do." Many times we want God to do it for us. I'm sorry, but there isn't any Holy Amnesia.

The one way I was able to let go of the past was to realize that God is a perfect parent, and Adam and Eve—His children—sinned and disobeyed. What a great day it was for me when the Lord spoke this softly into my heart. All humans have made mistakes. We have all done things we have regretted. God forgives much. I have had to learn to release much forgiveness concerning my childhood.

Pain from the Past

Growing up, I developed a severe weight problem. Words alone could never describe the pain of being fat as a child. Not only was there pain outside the home—other children can be so cruel—there was pain from inside the home as well. My mother did everything she could to motivate me to lose weight, but no matter how many diets I tried, I continued to gain weight. Mom thought that if she could shake me up, or shame me into action, perhaps she could spare me. I don't think she ever realized how painful her criticism was to me—how deeply it cut.

I remember our shopping together for an Easter outfit one year. In those days we didn't have Lane Bryant, 14 Plus, and all the other stores that cater to larger sizes. Our department store kept the Chubbet department hidden far in the back of the upper level. The clothes were all overpriced and very unattractive. My mother began to yell at me about my size, saying that she could get two or three outfits for the same price if I was normal. She yelled and I cried. In the heat of her anger, she called me a fat slob. That really hurt. Instead of Easter being a special holiday to me, it was a nightmare because it meant we had to buy new clothes.

I don't want to get very descriptive regarding the pain of my past, but I can tell you I had very low self-esteem. Although people always commented that I had such a pretty face, I thought they were just trying to be nice to the fat kid. I never felt pretty—I never even felt attractive.

During one of my attempts to fit in and feel accepted, I bought into the latest fad. It was the 1960s and mohair sweaters were all the rage. I wanted one so badly that I begged my parents for a sweater, saying it was all I wanted for Christmas. My parents fulfilled my Christmas wish; under the tree was a beautiful pink sweater, a matching skirt, and a lovely white blouse with a Peter Pan collar.

I still remember getting ready for school the morning after our Christmas vacation was over. I've never been more thankful for the cold weather of January. My new outfit was so soft and warm. It was perfect. As I walked to the bus stop, I actually felt pretty. My mother had even allowed me to wear a little lip gloss. My excitement simmered all through the bus ride because once I got to school, I would take off my bulky winter coat, and there would be this pretty girl all dressed in pink.

My memories are so vivid of the joy I felt as I approached my first class that morning. A song from the Broadway musical *West Side Story* best describes what was in my heart that day: "I feel pretty, Oh so pretty!" My happy anticipation peaked as I opened the classroom door and entered. That moment of intense joy was shattered as one of the young men in my class saw me and yelled, "Oh my God! It's a pink elephant!" Roars of laughter erupted from my classmates. They just howled over his joke, but it was all I could do not to cry. I swallowed hard all through that day— and for many years I continued to feel a large lump in my throat when I relived that memory.

Traveling home on the bus late that afternoon, I was thankful to have my winter coat on because it was shielding me from any additional witty remarks and painful comments on my looks. As a heavy child, I have other such memories that seem to be indelibly etched in my mind and heart. I still know the name of the boy who mocked me that day. I know the class, the time, the teacher. The wormwood and the gall are good images for the misery and bad treatment I experienced. After all, when we swallow the gall of bitterness, it has the poisonous effect of keeping those unhappy memories very fresh.

How is it then that during my visit with my brother Dirk, I thought of our childhood as being a balanced and healthy one? Even though I was tormented by bitter memories of insulting remarks concerning my weight, I had felt the need to deny any other family problems. I actually created a false picture in my mind in which my parents could have been Ozzie and Harriet Nelson—if you remember that TV show with its happy and well-adjusted parents and children. In reality, there were times of anger, violence, and fighting in my childhood. I loved my parents, but the truth is that their alcohol abuse made our home anything but happy.

He Is Able!

The verses in Lamentations, quoted at the beginning of this chapter, became very enlightening to me. I finally admitted how much gall and bitterness I had, and I longed for healing from acutely painful memories. Pretty in pink? Do you know, as I reflected on this traumatic event from the past and asked the Lord to heal me, He showed me that for over 25 years, I had never worn anything pink. In fact, I wouldn't even wear a sweater! Thank God I no longer have a visible weight problem and that I was able to lose over 100 pounds—not just once, but twice in my life! Yet in my mind, I still felt vulnerable.

We have a God of whom it is written, *"Now to him who is able to do immeasurable more than all we ask or imagine, according to his power that is at work within us, to him be glory in the church and in Christ Jesus through-out all generations, for ever and ever! Amen"* (Ephesians 3:20,21). I need to echo that last word: Amen! God provided healing when I asked for it. At least, the healing began when I asked Him to change my heart. Please notice that when I asked God to change my heart and to bring healing, He did so. In fact, His Holy Spirit was certainly speaking to my heart all along to *enable* me to ask for healing. What a faithful and gracious God He is!

When my son, Matthew, announced he was going to be married, I sensed that I was to wear a pink gown, as the Mother of the Groom. Only the Spirit of the Lord could have put such an idea into my heart and also given me the courage to follow through. I wanted to be free from the pain of my past, so my search began for a pink gown.

This was not an easy assignment. I went to every bridal salon in our area. I even drove to neighboring cities and couldn't find any dress that was right for me. I began to wonder if I had really heard from God. Did the dress really have to be pink? Our God "works in mysterious ways His wonders to perform." What a wonder He was about to perform for me.

A large church some distance from my home invited me to minister to their youth group. I accepted and arrangements were made for me and for my traveling companion, Jeannie Sink, to arrive early and stay at the home of the Pastor. His wife welcomed us into their beautiful home with real warmth and Christian love. She showed us to her guestroom and then left us to unpack. When I opened the closet door in this spare bedroom, I was startled to see several gowns in clear storage bags. Hanging directly in front of me was a lovely pink gown. The instant I saw the dress, I turned to Jeannie and announced "There's the gown for Matt's wedding."

We both began to laugh, but Jeannie didn't realize that I was serious. She was probably laughing because I had been complaining earlier about the prices of the gowns I had seen in the stores. Jean soon caught on that I was serious when I asked her to pray with me about this issue. I knew this was the gown, but how do you arrive in an unfamiliar pastor's house and tell his wife you want her gown? As we dressed for church that night, I waited to see how the Lord would provide the answer.

After the ministry of the Word that evening, I noticed the pastor's wife observing my tape table on display in the lobby. I walked over to her and told her to take a set of each. She was a little shocked as there were over 50 sets. I told her that I believed in what the Bible teaches about "what we sow we will also reap," and "it is more blessed to give than to receive." She asked me if there was something she could give me or do for me in return. This was my opportunity. "Well, since you asked," I said, "I couldn't help but notice the exquisite gowns in storage in the guest room closet. The pink one really caught my eye. Please forgive my boldness, and don't be offended, but my son is getting married and I have been looking for a pink gown to wear to his wedding. I haven't had any success, though. Would you even consider allowing me to borrow it just for that day? I promise to dry clean it and I'll see to it that every pearl and rhinestone stays intact..."

To my amazement and delight, she told me that I could try on the dress when we got home from the service. I have to say that all the way home, I was like a little girl full of giggles. I just knew that the dress would look beautiful on me. When I tried on the dress, we discovered it was a perfect fit: perfect length, size, *and* style. It was as though the gown had been made for me. Checking my calendar, I determined that I could drive back and pick up the dress a day or two before the wedding—then have it cleaned and returned right after the ceremony.

Jean and I were both so excited about the dress that we found it difficult to go to sleep. We were still awake when around midnight there was a soft knock on the bedroom door. It was the pastor's wife. She said that she had shared the story of the dress with her husband. Immediately I froze, thinking he had told her that she shouldn't be loaning her clothes. To my utter amazement, she announced that he had told her to give me the dress.

Tears of gratitude ran down my cheeks there in the dark—not only for this wonderful couple who had just blessed me, but also for my Heavenly Father who demonstrated His desire to replace my past misery and affliction with His favor and approval.

I felt very beautiful in my new pink gown at my son's wedding. I was on the lookout all that evening for a pink elephant, and there wasn't one to be found.

This dress represented a wonderful gift from the Lord, and so I have kept it ever since as a special trust. It hangs in my guestroom closet, waiting for another wounded little girl in a woman's body—a girl who needs to realize that she is not only pretty, but of great value, regardless of her outward appearance. This girl will have to learn that her worth and esteem come from the love of Jesus.

What a wonderful Lord we serve! Yet, when we are consumed with bitterness, we have lost all hope. When Jeremiah's heart had been filled with the wormwood and the gall, he expressed great despair: *"And I said My strength and my hope is perished from the Lord"* (Lamentations 3:18). Going back to Strong's we find that the word *strength* can also be translated "my goal." The Lexical Aids to the Greek-Hebrew Old Testament links the word *hope* to "expectations." When we are poisoned by the wormwood and gall of bitterness, we can lose all hope for the future and not bother to set goals. Our only expectations are for more trouble, loss, and mistreatment. This is a sad state to be in. In fact, although verse 19 uses the term *affliction,* the root for that word is *depression.* I think that as we counsel people who are depressed, we should first ascertain that there is no physical condition causing the depression. Next, though, we should pray to uncover roots of bitterness.

Bound by Iniquity

There is a New Testament example of a man who was not free until his bitterness was uncovered. The man's name is Simon. We read about him in Acts eight, and his story is a warning to all of us.

Philip the Evangelist held a great revival crusade in the town of Samaria. Many people were saved, healed, and/or delivered. In this same town was a well-known man named Simon. He was a sorcerer who had bewitched the city. All the people held him in high esteem and thought his power came from God; however, the Bible forbids us to be involved in the occult, sorcery, magic, and the like. (See Deuteronomy 18:10; Exodus 22:18; Isaiah 47:9,12,13; Malachi 3:5; 2 Chronicles 33:6; Acts 16:16; Galatians 5:20; Revelation 21:8; 22:15.) If Simon were with us today, he would have a psychic hotline: 1-900-04MONEY. That's the kind of man he was. The good news is that when the people of Samaria heard Philip, they believed what he said about the kingdom of God. Even Simon believed and was baptized. The Word says *"he continued with Philip, and wondered beholding the miracles and signs which were done"* (Acts 8:13b).

When the apostles heard about what was happening in Samaria, they sent Peter and John as reinforcements. *"Who, when they were come down, prayed for them, that they might receive the Holy Ghost: (For as yet he was fallen upon none of them: only they were baptized in the name of the Lord Jesus.) Then laid they their hands on them, and they received the Holy Ghost. And when Simon saw that through laying on of the apostles' hands the Holy Ghost was given, he offered them money"* (Acts 8:15-18).

The Holy Spirit is a gift from God, and this gift is never for sale at any price. The apostles sharply rebuked Simon for even thinking such a thing. Now, keep in mind that Simon was known as a real somebody in that town. He had a great deal of pride in his heart and didn't want to lose his important position in the community. It would be humiliating for him to be publicly corrected like this, yet Peter's next words cut to the very core of the issue and pierced Simon's heart: *"Thou hast neither part nor lot in this matter: for thy heart is not right in the sight of God. Repent therefore of this thy wickedness, and pray God, if perhaps the thought of thine heart may be forgiven thee. For I perceive that thou art in the gall of bitterness, and in the bond of iniquity"* (Acts 8: 21-23). The New King James Version says, *"For I see that you are poisoned by bitterness and bound by iniquity"* (v.23).

Simon's response came quickly and humbly: *"Pray ye to the Lord for me, that none of these things which ye have spoken come upon me."* (Acts 8:24).

How did Peter see into Simon's heart? I believe he could tell that Simon's motivation was wrong initially because of the words of his mouth. Notice that Peter said Simon was in the gall of bitterness, or the poison of bitterness, and thus was bound up or in a bond forged by iniquity or wickedness. We need to see clearly that bitterness poisons us, so that we will be eager, rather than reluctant, to repent and seek forgiveness. Did you know that when a chicken is "dressed," —or undressed would be more logical since we're talking about the innards being removed—a sack of gall must be removed from near the chicken's tail? Check your favorite old-fashioned cookbook that describes in detail how to prepare a chicken from plucking the feathers to roasting in the oven. Somewhere in the directions, you'll find a warning that if the gall sack is not removed, the entire chicken will be bitter and inedible. Do we want our bitterness to make us unusable for God's kingdom? Absolutely not! Don't let yourself be trapped by trying to pass the blame: "But you don't know what this person did to me. I can never forgive what they did." Well, let me remind you that God forgave you plenty—you did more to offend His holiness than anyone else could have done to offend you. Jesus said that since God forgave us, we also *have* to forgive others who have sinned against us. In fact, He said—and I'll quote from the New King James Version so there can be no chance you'll misunderstand His direction— *"But if you do not forgive men their trespasses, neither will your Father forgive your trespasses"* (Matthew 6:15). Think about that.

Some of us may still be in denial regarding our having any bitterness. I know I have been on many occasions. Bitterness doesn't have to be a permanent condition or personality type, but it surely has an unattractive sound. We'd rather say we're a little irritable or that we're "dealing with something," but until we're honest about the extent of our sin, we won't ask for release and freedom. If we regard bitterness with the seriousness that God does, we will surely be quicker to identify the bitterness and stay away from it.

A Poisonous Tone
Let's back up to Acts 8:23 and take a close look at the origin of the

Greek word that is translated *bitterness*. The root is from a word meaning acridity, piercing, sharp, pungent (especially Poison), according to *Strong's Concordance*. It was Simon's words *and the way he said them* that alerted Peter to the piercing, sharp, and cutting nature of his feelings.

How many times have we been stung, cut, or pierced by the words of another? And how many times do our own words contain a barb for someone else? This is one way we can begin to judge if we have bitterness towards anyone. Oh, we may be quick to say, "I forgive you," when someone has hurt us; but how do we really feel? Have we gone through the process needed to bring the forgiveness into our hearts? How do you talk to others about the situation or the person involved? Is there any acid in your speech?

At times I have heard myself speak with such sharpness it surprised me. Sometimes a spouse, a good friend, or the Holy Spirit will be the one that notices the sharpness and brings it to our attention. When cutting remarks or sharp words are spoken, we need to look into our hearts. Whatever it is that we are "doing for the Lord," can that action be more important and urgent than *being* what we need to be in the Lord? You may have heard this reminder before, but God created us as human *beings*—not human *doings*. What we are before God is more important than what we do, and what's in our hearts is most important of all. Can our hearts be a fit dwelling place for Christ?

When we discover the poison of gall and wormwood within us, we need to follow the advice given to Simon: Repent and pray to the Lord for forgiveness. He is utterly faithful to cleanse and to forgive.

How About You

1. Since we can't alter our childhood, how can we make the most of our life now?

2. Do you believe that the Lord can heal the emotional pains from your childhood?

3. Ask the Holy Spirit to tell you which memories need to be healed.

4. Is there anyone you haven't fully forgiven?

5. Was there ever a time you made fun of someone else? Do you now regret that mocking? As the Holy Spirit brings them to mind, pray for each person you may have wounded by your words or tone of voice.

Bitter Words

The Bible has much to say about the life that comes through obeying the words of the Lord. It also speaks of the power that resides in the words we speak. Our words can bring healing and blessing, or our words can wound. You've heard of character assassination. Isn't that killing someone's reputation by the words you share? The wise man had this to say: *"Life and death are in the power of the tongue"* (Proverbs 18:21a). I like the way The Message renders this verse because it's so blunt: *"Words kill, words give life; they're either poison or fruit—you choose."*

"Sticks and stones can break my bones, but words will never hurt me." Children sing this rhyme, but I doubt if many of them believe it. We recover much more quickly from the flesh wounds that sticks and stones inflict than we do from the internal damage of cutting and bitter words. Even broken bones usually heal faster than wounded feelings. Children may try to defend themselves from insults by singing this rhyme. They may even temporarily believe that it is some kind of magical chant that blocks the pain of unkind words, but the truth is that cruel words often do hurt us.

What do the words we speak really tell others about us? We saw in the last chapter that Simon's bitterness of heart was revealed to Peter because of the words Simon spoke. I firmly believe that the tone of voice used plays just as big a part in revealing what we truly mean as the words we actually say. It is my prayer for all of us that we be able to discern when bitterness of heart and gall are present, and that by this discernment we may be able to save ourselves some pain.

Peter told Simon that he—Simon—was in the bond of iniquity. This is an unusual phrase to use, but it's Biblical. Look at Psalm 64. *"Hide me from the secret counsel of the wicked; from the insurrection of the workers of iniquity: Who whet their tongue like a sword and bend their bows to shoot their arrows, even bitter words"* (v.2,3). The Psalmist prays to be hidden from the workers of iniquity. Why? Because they speak bitter words, and when bitter words come, they are as arrows shot from a bow. Sticks and stones may break my bones, but bitter words are like being shot by arrows. The Amplified version translates verse 3 in this way: *"Who whet their tongues like a sword, who aim venomous words like arrows."* Does it sound to you like those workers of iniquity plan to hurt others with their words? It does to me.

"The words of the wicked are to lie in wait for blood" (Proverbs 12:6). When you consider that the word *whet* means to sharpen for pointing and piercing, then yes, it seems even clearer that the wicked deliberately inflict wounds with their words. Some words cut us deeply right away, but other words seem to lie dormant within us—waiting to draw blood at some future occasion. *"For the lips of a strange woman drop as a honeycomb, and her mouth is smoother than oil; But her end is bitter as wormwood, sharp as a two-edged sword"* (Proverbs 5:3,4).

Smooth as oil, but bitter in the end. There are times when a person who has bitterness towards you will speak in a soft and smooth fashion. Their words melt like butter—initially, that is. In the end, they have a bitter bite. I experienced this when I was a young girl. It seemed as though bitter words would lie in wait to draw my blood. Even years later, the old wounds can reopen and we can begin to bleed all over again.

Surprising Prize

An instance from my childhood will illustrate this issue. I don't recall my exact age, but I think I was around eight or nine years old when something very exciting happened in our quiet little neighborhood. I grew up in a town called Pleasantville, and our neighbors were pleasant people. I played many games with the kids on our block, and in those days, everyone knew each other. I could tell you the names of every person who lived on our street, and even several streets over as well. We always addressed the adults as Mr. and Mrs.

Things have really changed since I was a child. We kids were allowed outside until it got dark, playing kick the can, and hide and seek. I don't remember hearing of a child being abducted in those days. We never even locked our doors. In fact, on many a summer night, the neighbors would all leave front doors wide open, with just the screen doors for a barrier. The heat and humidity were more of a problem than intruders, and we expected that anyone who came to the door would be welcome. If there was a knock at the door, we didn't look through a peephole. We didn't look at all, usually; we just hollered, "Come in!" Yes, times have changed.

Back to the exciting thing that happened. I was good friends with the girl who lived two houses over from me. We played with dolls together, and when it would rain and we couldn't play outside we played cards inside. We usually started with "Go Fish," but when we got tired of that, we'd move to the more aggressive game of "War." While playing cards, we'd often listen to the local radio station. This was exciting because they ran frequent giveaway programs as promotions, and Carol was the type of girl who would always call in to solve a riddle or name a tune. Consequently, when a new contest was announced for which the grand prize-winner of the "Name the Chocolate Sauce" would win a *horse,* Carol quickly filled out her postcard and sent it in. There must have been millions of entries because this kind of grand prize was enormous, gigantic in the eyes of a child—but Carol won! We ran door to door, sharing the exciting news that Carol had won a horse, a real live horse.

I remember taking pony rides at the 4-H Fair, but all of us kids had to stand in such long lines—and even then the rides weren't free. Mom and Dad had to pay and for what! All the horse did was go in circles, never a trot or a gallop—just a plodding walk. And when you dismounted, you better be careful where you stepped. In my eyes, Carol's prize was about the best thing that ever happened. Every detail seemed to work out for her. We didn't have any stables near us, and the closest zoo was almost an hour away; but Carol's father told us they were going to turn their garage into a barn. Good-bye car rides; hello Zorro!

It seemed like months before they were able to turn the garage into a stable, but that was probably due to our intense anticipation. Every day seemed endless as we waited for the horse to arrive. I even helped stack the bales of hay in preparation for the big event. Finally, the horse trailer pulled up at the curb and we all stood watching with bated breath.

The horse was beautiful—a deep chocolate brown. I never knew there were so many kids in our neighborhood. They seemed to come out of the woodwork just to see this wonderful horse. We were all sent home that first day, and many children were deeply disappointed. I wasn't really sad at all because I had the twin advantages of living so close *and* being one of Carol's best friends. Her dad told all of us that if we came back on Saturday morning, he would give each of us a ride.

As you can imagine, I had trouble sleeping that Friday night. I just kept waking up. I was filled with enthusiasm and happiness, not just for myself, but for my girlfriend, Carol. I had visions of riding lessons and myself looking like Liz Taylor in *National Velvet*. There was only one problem with my visions. I was indeed young enough, but jockeys have to be short and thin. I met the height requirement, being short enough; but the weight requirement was a whole other thing, since I was on the heavy side.

Messages that Make Us Fearful

Saturday morning finally arrived, and all of us kids made a long line out past our neighbors' fence onto the sidewalk. I waited and waited. Everybody was having such a great time that it wasn't that hard to wait. It was so nice of Carol's dad to spend his day off lifting one kid after another onto the horse, teaching them how to sit in the saddle and how to hold the reins.

After what seemed like an eternity, I was next in line. I approached, smiling at Carol's dad and ready to be instructed on how to mount the horse. He looked at me and grinned, but the next words out of his mouth just devastated me. "You can't ride this horse, Gwen. You're so fat you'll break its back!" I stared at him in disbelief for a moment, and then as laughter erupted behind me, I turned and fled to the shelter of my home.

By the time I reached my house, I was sobbing so hard I was out of control. How could he say that to me in front of all the other kids? What had I ever done to him that he could be so mean to me? I realized he meant it as a joke, but it certainly wasn't funny to me. I was crushed that day, the weight of his words heavier than I could bear.

Didn't he realize that his remark was not humorous but humiliating? Those words struck me as if I had been shot with an arrow. Later on he said he had meant no harm; he was only joking. He even wanted to know where my sense of humor was. I tried to laugh along on the outside and say it was okay, but on the inside I didn't think it was funny at all.

I'm not the first person who has been hurt by some misplaced humor. Many have been wounded by a so-called "funny remark" at their expense. These hurts are difficult to get over, and the bitter words often lie in wait to draw blood.

A few years later I was in Girl Scouts, and one of our first outings as a troop was for all of us to go horseback riding together. I wasn't going to be a little girl in line anymore. I was now a young lady in my teens. I felt enough time had passed since the earlier horse episode that I could now enjoy this event. I knew even though I was an overweight young adult, it would not be a problem for the horse to carry me. But, when we got to the stables, the memories came flooding back and I was filled with misgivings. "You're so fat you'll break the horse's back," rang in my ears. Logically, I knew this wasn't true, but my heart was not so sure.

I don't even want to share with you what happened that day at the stables. When I finally mustered the courage to mount the horse, I stood on the block and put my left foot into the stirrup. I intended to swing my right leg over the saddle, but when I just started to put my weight on the stirrup, the saddle slipped under the horse's belly. It seems the girth wasn't cinched tightly enough. This could only happen to me. I heard more laughter, wiped away more tears, and swallowed more bitterness.

I was not a happy camper when, after becoming a Christian in 1974, I read in the Scriptures that when Jesus returns He will be riding a white horse. In Revelation we read that His servants will be clothed in fine white linen, and they will be His army, following after Him on horseback. That's a picture of real victory, and yet all I could think was *Jesus, please help me. I can't ride!* Bitter experiences of the past can make us very fearful.

"My soul is among lions; and I lie even among them that are set on fire, even the sons of men, whose teeth are spears and arrows, and their tongue a sharp sword" (Psalm 57:4). The New Testament gives us insight as to the identity of the lion that would shoot bitter arrows at us. *"Be sober, be vigilant; because your adversary, the devil, as a roaring lion, walketh about, seeking whom he may devour"* (1 Peter 5:8). This certainly sheds some light on who the lion is in Psalm 57. The arrows he uses to afflict us are often the arrows of bitter words.

Even so the tongue is a little member and boasteth great things. Behold how great a matter a little fire kindleth, and the tongue is a fire, a world of iniquity, so is the tongue among our members, that it defileth the whole body, and setteth on fire the course of nature; and it is set on fire of hell. For every kind of beasts and of birds and of <u>serpents</u>, and of things in the sea, is tamed, and hath been tamed of mankind; But the tongue can no man tame; it is an unruly evil, full of deadly <u>poison</u> (James 3:5-8, emphasis added).

Whew! Why didn't James say what he *really* thought! We have to know the serious consequences of the words we speak. When we share bitter words, we are really releasing poison. Furthermore, we see that although it is possible for us to tame all sorts of animals, we can't tame our tongue. When we read that the tongue "is set on fire of hell," we know where the bitter words are coming from. Satan is out to devour us. Jesus also said *"The thief cometh not, but for to steal, and to kill, and to destroy; I am come that they might have life, and that they might have it more abundantly"* (John 10:10). Most commentators assume the thief Jesus refers to is the devil. In another description of the enemy, Jesus said, *"He was a murderer from the beginning, and abode not in the truth, because there is no truth in him. When he speaketh a lie, he speaketh of his own: for he is a liar, and the father of it"* (John 8:44b). Don't misunderstand me. We do have a responsibility for our actions and our words, but our ancient enemy, the devil, works against us to keep us from being effective witnesses in our community. What better way than to tempt us to slander each other, shooting those bitter-word arrows that poison our victims.

When Our Words Are Weapons

There are other scripture verses that describe the terrible things our words can do. *"They have sharpened their tongues like a serpent, adders poison is under their lips"* (Psalm 140:3). The same verse in the New International Version reads this way: *"They sharpen their tongues as a serpent; Poison of a viper is under their tongues."* When we are hit with the arrows of poisonous words, filled with gall and bitterness, we have been bitten by the serpent.

Many of us have attended workshops on spiritual warfare. We've been taught a great deal about how to fight the good fight of faith. Scripture says we are to submit to God, to resist the devil and he will flee. This is absolutely true, of course. But one of the weapons we find the most harmful is the weapon of our very own words. Satan is skilled at prompting us to say things that are hurtful or to take offense at the words of others. Since I have come to the Lord, it has been other believers who have wounded me by their words. I have been pierced and can testify personally that the verses in Psalms are true. A tongue can be like a sword that has been dipped in poison.

So, what can we do to fight effectually for the Lord instead of hurting each other? Let's consider the armor of God, which is listed in the book of Ephesians. This is a familiar passage to most of us:

> *Therefore, take up the full armor of God, so that you will be able to resist in the evil day, and having done everything to stand firm. Stand firm therefore, having girded your loins with truth, and having put on the breastplate of righteousness, and having shod your feet with the preparation of the gospel of peace; in addition to all, taking up the shield of faith with which you will be <u>able to extinguish all the flaming arrows of the evil one</u>. And take the helmet of salvation, and the sword of the Spirit, which is the word of God. With all prayer and petition, pray at all times in the Spirit, and with this in view, be on the alert with all perseverance and petition for all the saints...* (Ephesians 6:13-18, New American Standard Version, emphasis added).

I studied the whole armor of God soon after I became a Christian and felt confident that I knew each piece. Then, several years ago, I was privileged to go to the Virgin Islands and minister at a women's retreat. One of the other guest speakers asked this question of everyone in the audience: "Who can name for us the armor of God?" I put my hand up nice and high and was called on to answer the question. I stood at my seat and began to recite the armor found in the book of Ephesians.

In a loud, strong, confident voice, I listed the armor. "First we have the girdle of truth, next is the breastplate, followed by the shoes on our feet. We carry the shield, and then there's the helmet, and of course, the sword." Tada! The speaker politely thanked me, but she said that I was incorrect and would I please be seated.

I sat down feeling very surprised. My mind raced through the familiar verses in Ephesians. Was the mistake the order in which I had listed them? The speaker began to share something then that has been of extreme value to me, and I am so glad that I can share it with you. We have been making the symbol of the armor the focus of our attention, and thereby we have missed the actual armor.

Paul was in prison when he wrote to the church at Ephesus. The most common daily sights for him at this time were the many Roman guards stationed throughout the prison. From seeing them and from the inspiration of the Holy Spirit, he drew the picture of the armor that God provides for us. The description includes the helmet, the sword, the shield, etc. But the helmet, the sword, and so forth are not the real armor. They only help us form a picture so that we can focus on the real armor.

Therefore, the first piece mentioned is not the belt or girdle but the truth! The next item is not the breastplate, but the righteousness God supplies. You see that when we have looked at the real armor of God, we find it is truth, righteousness, peace, faith, salvation, and the Word. We have had our focus diverted to dwell on the symbol of the armor and not the substance of the true armor. This may have caused us to stop short in our listing of armor and exclude pieces that are included in verse 18. *"Praying always with all prayer and supplication in the Spirit, and watching thereonto with all perseverance and supplication for all the saints"* Two important pieces of the armor are *prayer* and *watching*.

When we are in prayer and when we are watching, we are not blindsided, taken by surprise. Spending time in the Word builds our faith and it is the shield of faith which extinguishes the flaming arrows of the evil one. And what do these arrows represent most often? Bitter words that pierce and wound. God provides faith as a gift to us—a gift we need in order to stand firm in this battle. Thank God for the shield of faith.

Protecting His Reputation

I only had two real fights growing up, and I was forced to fight both times. One of my fights was with a girl named Joan. She was a real bully, and everyone was afraid of her, including yours truly. She particularly used to pick on me on Saturday mornings when my Mom dropped my friends and me off at the matinee at our local movie theater. For a quarter we got two cartoons, and a full-length movie. (I guess that dates me all right!) Well, Joan used to pick on me, take my candy money, and call me names. I was too scared to stand up to her, so this abuse continued Saturday after Saturday.

But on one Saturday morning she finally crossed the line. I had allowed her to bully me and call me names, but on this particular morning, she called my father a name. That was it. I told her to put on the gloves and go outside. We left the theater and word spread from aisle to aisle, "There's a fight outside in the alley!" Who wanted to watch cartoons when there was a real fight? All the kids gathered to see the bully beat up the wimp. Were they ever surprised! When we began to fight, Joan didn't stand a chance. I kicked, I bit, I scratched, I spit, I screamed, and I hit. They had to pull me off her. Now I am not using this illustration to say that we should "fight dirty," but I am saying we should give it all we've got.

I guess you know I didn't have any more trouble at the movies or from Joan. What was it that day that made me finally stand firm? She attacked my father. Saints, we have a Father whose name and reputation must be protected. We are in a battle, like it or not; and it's time to draw the line and to use our faith, lifting up the shield against every arrow of the wicked one.

Maybe as a child you were called names, or told that you were stupid, or that you would never amount to anything. The flaming arrows of these bitter words may have caused wounds that are still burning away, and it's time they were extinguished. Lift your shield of faith by finding promises in the Word of God, promises concerning His love for you that counted you worthy of His Son dying for you on the cross. That is an everlasting and amazing love. The Eternal Father has set His affection upon you. Doesn't that build your faith into a shield that protects you from Satan's fiery missiles?

In the Old Testament times, the shields were much larger than the ones we usually envision, the ones from the knights in the Middle Ages. In Bible times, the shields were big enough to do a lot of good, especially when they were being held over the head to protect against a rain of flaming arrows shot from an enemy stronghold. Why does this make a difference to us? Well, consider this. Since the battle is fought in our minds, we are told to take every thought captive and bring it to the obedience of Christ.

In order to do this, the Word tells us we need to be renewed in the spirit of our minds. "*And be not conformed to this world, but be ye transformed by the renewing of your mind*" (Romans 12:2). Men feel pressure to perform, and women feel pressure to conform; but the Lord wants all of us transformed. Can you see how salvation can be likened to a helmet that protects our heads, and how faith assists the helmet to render those arrows powerless to hurt us?

Speaking Words of Life

"*There is that speaketh like the piercings of a sword; but the tongue of the wise is health*" (Proverbs 12:18). Begin to speak health to yourself. Don't agree with words sent to attack you, bitter words that lie in wait to draw blood. Remember that the blood of Jesus brought healing for us and the words of the wise are health. We read earlier that life and death are in the power of the tongue. Go ahead and speak life to your spirit. Go to the Lord and be healed of those old wounds that are still dripping blood.

There's a story in the gospels of a woman who had an issue of blood for twelve years. She heard of Jesus, and believing in Him, she pressed through the crowd to touch Him. She thought that if she only touched the hem of His garment, she would be healed. One day as I was reading this familiar story, the Spirit of the Lord spoke to my heart that He wanted to heal my issues of blood. Do you also have bitter memories that are causing you to bleed? No one else may be able to see them, but you know they are there. When God spoke to me, I knew immediately one issue of blood in my heart that He wanted to heal. You see, growing up, my younger brother and I had many conflicts. In the course of our bickering, many mean and bitter words were spoken. Arrows flew freely, and we both suffered a great deal of pain in our relationship. We had been estranged for many, many years by too many bitter memories, too many bitter words.

When the Lord spoke to me, I knew that if I could just press in and touch Jesus, I too could be healed. The woman in the Gospel account knew right away within her body that she had been healed of whatever plague was causing her to bleed. When the Lord healed me, I felt in my body that I had been delivered from the plague that had so distanced me from my baby brother. I can still remember the past, but when I remember it I don't relive it.

I have been healed of many issues of blood, praise the Lord. Many bitter words from the past have lost their sting. The Word of God, Jesus Himself, has been that word of life to me in each of these situations. Because He was wounded for my transgressions, willingly shedding His blood that I might be set free, I sing with new understanding that old hymn, "Oh the Blood of Jesus, that washes white as snow..."

How About You?

1. When is the last time someone's words hurt you? Have you forgiven that person?

2. Ask your spouse or a friend to tell you when your words are sharp and bitter? Do you notice a pattern?

3. How do you lift the shield of faith when bitter words are flying like arrows?

4. Since the tongue of the wise brings healing, what can you say to begin to mend your wounds? (Read James 1.)

Chapter 6

Gap in the Hedge

It's interesting that the devil has many names in the Scriptures. He's called Satan, Lucifer, the old dragon, the prince and the god of this world, the deceiver, and the tempter. We have also recently seen him called the wicked one, the father of lies, a thief, robber, and destroyer. However, the form we most strongly associate with him is that of a serpent.

We are initially introduced to him in Genesis in the Garden of Eden. In that gorgeous and wonderful paradise, he is the destructive element, the serpent in the Garden. We can easily picture him as a snake in the grass, slithering around under cover. He is sly, cautious, subtle, and he is just waiting to attack. Not a very victorious picture, but it's important for us to realize that there will be few blatant and obvious attacks on us. Temptation is more likely to be appealing if it's gradual rather than sudden. Remember our armor? We have to watch and pray. We have to be on guard. This is warfare of a subtle kind.

The Bible has other clues about the power of the serpent. *"He that diggeth a pit shall fall into it, and whoso breaketh a hedge, a serpent shall bite him"* (Ecclesiastes 10:8). In verse 11 of this same chapter, we are told that the serpent will bite without enchantment. This means the serpent won't be charmed. We have all seen movies where a snake charmer plays his flute and hypnotizes the snake. When the snake is in a deep trance, it does whatever the snake charmer wants it to do. That may work in the movies or in cartoons, but in real life things are a bit different. The Word implies that if we have a gap or break in the hedge, no amount of charming will avail; the serpent will bite us. What does this mean?

Some snakes rattle or hiss in warning before striking their victims. Satan doesn't do that, but he can only attack if we let our guard down in some way or another. I'm speaking here, of course, of believers in Jesus. If we're not believers in Jesus, we've not only let our guard down, we don't even have a guard. So what is this hedge? When Satan contended with the Lord over God's servant, Job, you'll remember the devil said he couldn't attack Job because there was a hedge around him. *"Hast not thou made an hedge about him, and about his house, and about all that he hath on every side?"* (Job 1:10a). There is a clear picture here of God protecting Job and his family on every side. In fact, the word that is translated *hedge* in this text comes from a root meaning "to shut in and to restrain." Thank God we have a hedge around us on every side to restrain us and to shut us in. Even Satan knew he couldn't get to the man of God unless there was a gap in that hedge.

Job also realized that a hedge was about him, but he expressed it a bit differently. *"Why is light given to a man whose way is hid, and whom God hath hedged in?"* (Job 3:23). This hedge is not the same one as the hedge in chapter one. This hedge means to cover with a screen. Let me share a story with you that may help you to picture this kind of protection.

When I was a young girl we lived close to the shore. Our house had a large, screened front porch. On really hot summer nights, my brothers and I would fight as to who would be allowed to sleep on the front porch. The screens allowed the wonderful sea breezes to come in, but protected us from all the bugs and mosquitoes. One summer our relatives from Ohio came to visit us. We didn't have enough bedrooms for all of them, so two of my cousins slept on the front porch: one in a hammock, and the other on the swing. Little did we know that one of my cousins was a sleepwalker. The poor guy didn't wake up until he had pushed through the screen and had fallen off the porch into our sticker bushes. He woke up then, and he woke everyone else up, too, with his hollering.

My cousin had plenty of scratches, cuts, and gnat bites, but the part of him that really suffered was his pride. His injuries made me vividly aware that the screens were a good protection for us. Only when he broke through the "hedge of screens" did harm come to him.

Standing in the Day of Battle

There is another meaning for the word hedge beyond these meanings of to shut in, to restrain, or to screen. The meaning of the word *hedge* as used in Ecclesiastes 10:8 is to surround with a wall. So if God has put a hedge around us to shut us in for restraint, to cover us as with a screen or to surround with a wall of protection, how is it that the serpent can find a gap and attack us? The answer to this question occurred to me one day at a women's retreat at Mt. Misery, of all places. My eyes were opened to a truth I had missed every time I read the book of Job. Remember that the Lord allowed Satan to afflict Job, and one of the main problems Job had was that he didn't understand who his enemy was. God was still for him; it was Satan who afflicted him. Job asked why light was given to him whose way is hid.

Until the light was revealed to Job, he did not understand that he needed to be delivered from the hand of the enemy. In Chapter 6:22-24, Job asks God to teach him and show him where he had erred. Notice he does not ask to be delivered. He still thinks of God as the enemy, and to be honest, there are times when we think this, too. We may not realize we're thinking this, but our doubts and fears are evidence that we don't fully trust God.

Let's consider this in relation to the hedge. When there is a gap or break in a hedge or wall, opportunity arises for an enemy to attack—particularly a subtle enemy who is always looking for a breach in the wall or a gap in the hedge.

> *And the word of the Lord came unto me saying, Son of man, prophesy against the prophets of Israel that prophesy, and say thou unto them that prophesy out of their own hearts, Hear ye the word of the Lord. Thus saith the Lord God: Woe unto the foolish prophets that follow their own spirit, and have seen nothing! O Israel, thy prophets are like the foxes in the deserts. Ye have not gone up into the gaps, neither made up the hedge for the house of Israel to stand in the battle in the day of the Lord* (Ezekiel 13:1-5).

To stand in the day of battle…that's the main reason for the hedge around us. We are in a battle, and God wants His house and His people to be able to stand. Do you see the connection between the language used in this verse and the verses in Ephesians 6? "*Having done all to stand, stand therefore.*" We know we are in a battle and that we have an enemy; the good news is that God wants us to stand and also to win. We're not just supposed to sing victory choruses, we should be experiencing victories in our lives, and not defeats. But according to the verses in Ezekiel, if we haven't gone up and filled in the gaps that have appeared in our hedges, we won't even be able to stand.

There's another verse in Ezekiel that talks about the gap in the hedge. This is a verse you may already know: "*And I sought for a man among them, that should make up the hedge, and stand in the gap before me for the land, that I should not destroy it; but I found none*" (Ezekiel 22:30). This refers to another sort of battle. God had looked among the prophets, the priests, the princes, and the peoples, looking for a man to stand in the gap. He didn't find one. I believe the Lord is still looking to see if we will stand in the gap, in order to make up the hedge in the day of battle. Add this to the verse in Ecclesiastes about the bite of the serpent, and we can see that it's time to go into the gardening business and in the spirit look for gaps and breaks in our hedges.

The Bible tells us what makes a break in the first place. "*Wherefore thus saith the Holy One of Israel, because ye despise this word, and trust in oppression and perverseness, and stay thereon: Therefore this iniquity shall be to you as a breach ready to fall, swelling out in a high wall, whose breaking cometh suddenly at an instant*" (Isaiah 30:12,13). According to the New International Version, "*this sin will become for you like a high wall, cracked and bulging, that collapses suddenly, in an instant.*" A sin or iniquity will cause a break in our hedge, opening the wall; and believe me, Satan won't wait for a second invitation to bite!

> *Why do we sit still? Assemble yourselves, and let us enter into the defensed cities, and let us be silent there: for the Lord our God hath put us to silence, and given us water of gall to drink because we have sinned against the Lord...For behold I will send serpents, cockatrices among you, which will not be charmed and they shall bite you, saith the Lord* (Jeremiah 8:14,17).

What is the difference between a serpent and a cockatrice? In other versions these words are translated as venomous snakes and vipers. The word serpent refers to a hissing creature. The word *cockatrice* stands for a viper that thrusts out his tongue. *Webster's New World Dictionary* defines cockatrice in the following way: "*1. A fabulous serpent supposedly hatched from a cock's egg and having power to kill by a look. 2. Bible (KJV) an unidentified deadly serpent.*"

The Serpent and the Curse

When the serpent had bitten Adam and Eve, in a manner of speaking—by causing them to sin—a curse was pronounced upon the serpent, but a promise was also made concerning the woman's seed. It's no wonder that most women hate snakes. When Eve sinned and disobeyed the voice of God, a penalty of this disobedience was that there would be enmity between her and the serpent. (See Genesis 3:15.) The promise in this passage concerns what the woman's seed would do to the serpent.

The seed of the woman will bruise the head of the serpent, and the serpent will bruise his heel. Satan has bruised many of God's children, but thank God for Jesus. He is the seed of the woman that came to destroy the works of the devil.

Now you may have been thinking, women don't supply the seed in procreation. Women have eggs and the men are given the seeds. This is one of the most important issues of the virgin birth. Men are the ones who produce the seed, but Mary, the mother of Jesus, had not known a man, in the Biblical sense. She was overshadowed by the Holy Spirit. The Babe within her was the Son of God. Jesus, the seed of God, was implanted in a woman. Therefore, the seed of the woman—that is, Jesus—would tread on the serpent's head.

"And the God of peace shall bruise Satan under your feet shortly" (Romans 16:20). Until Satan is put under our feet, once and for all by the God of peace, we will be in danger of snakebite—unless we are totally obedient to God. The sin of disobedience puts a gap in the hedge. How about Job who was supposed to be a righteous man? Many feel that his fears put a gap in his hedge. *"For the thing which I greatly feared is come upon me, and that which I was afraid of is come unto me"* (Job 3:25). Although the two words *feared* and *afraid* seem very similar in English, the lexical aids in my Bible tell me that the root of fear has to do with dread and alarm. The word *afraid* has to do with the expectation of punishment. Job goes on to say, *"I was not in safety, neither had I rest, neither was I quiet; yet trouble came"* (Job 3:26). I can only surmise from these verses that Job had some hidden fears. Even when things seemed to be going well around him, he didn't have quiet and rest within himself.

The Bondage of Fear

Do you have hidden fears that may be putting a gap in your hedge? For many years I was afraid of getting cancer. My mother came from a large family, and many of her brothers and sisters had cancer. She herself died of cancer in 1979. I thank God that she was a believer, but I regret that her life was cut short by this disease. She was only 59 when she died.

After her death, I began to confess according to the Word that I would not die of cancer.

I confessed that I would live long on the earth and show God's salvation. Even though I said this boldly on the outside, inside I lived in daily dread that cancer was somewhere in my body. You see, two of my aunts lived with us when I was a child. One had a mastectomy and the other a colostomy. One of their brothers had throat cancer and had to have a part of his tongue removed. Cancer was a common subject in our house from my earliest childhood on. When my mother died of cancer, I knew I had to be free from this fear or my life wouldn't be much worth living.

I began to study the Scriptures on healing and faith. Since faith comes by hearing, specifically hearing the Word of God, just by studying and repeating the Word, I was growing in faith. I was very concerned about the truths in the Bible regarding health and healing.

It was about this time that our church had a healing crusade. One night during the week of meetings, the speaker stated something that made me sit bolt upright in surprise. He had started telling us about his parents and how one of them had died of cancer. He also shared that he began confession in faith that he would not die of cancer. His next words impacted my life to a tremendous degree. He said that not only would he not die of cancer, but he wouldn't live the rest of his life with a spirit of fear of cancer.

A spirit of fear of cancer? I had read this somewhere in the Bible. Searching through the Word I found this: "*For God hath not given us the spirit of fear; but of power, and of love, and of a sound mind*" (2 Timothy 1:7). This was a familiar verse, but I had never before grasped the concept that fear could be a spirit. As the speaker continued to share this teaching with the audience, I began to shake and had the almost overwhelming need to cry. What was this? Did I have a spirit of fear of cancer? Could a believer have a spirit of fear within him? From that moment on, I just wanted the speaker to hurry and finish his message so that I could come forward for prayer. He seemed to take a long time to close, but when he finished his message, he opened the altar area for people who wanted to receive ministry. I didn't even wait for him to conclude his invitation before I was asking people to please excuse me, I needed to get to the front of the church right away. I stood by the altar waiting for ministry, not knowing what to expect. In my heart I just asked over and over, "Dear Jesus, please help me!"

Deliverance for a Christian? My head wasn't accepting this very well, but my heart told me that I was where I needed to be. My body was shaking and I was gripped with fear. When the man of God approached me, I could only say, "Cancer... fear... fear cancer." He took authority over the spirit of fear of cancer.

I am a little embarrassed to share what happened next, but much stranger stuff is in print than what happened to me and to him. When the power of God touched me, I let out a sob and my head ended up on his shoulder as I cried and cried. The only problem is that with my uncontrollable crying came snotting. When I lifted my head finally to celebrate my newfound freedom, I was shocked and horrified to see what I had just done to his beautiful suit jacket. You guessed it. What should have been deposited in a handkerchief was displayed unmistakably for all to see.

Some kind soul from the congregation jumped up and draped a clean handkerchief over the speaker's shoulder, and he just continued to minister. The next thing I knew, one of the women from the church was holding me and praying, thanking Jesus for my deliverance. After I regained my composure and the service ended, I walked over to our guest speaker. Most of the people had left and in the back of the auditorium I could quietly tell him how sorry I was about the accident with his coat. I even handed him $5.00 to have his jacket cleaned. I was happy to have a few moments to speak with him because I didn't really understand what had just happened to me. The speaker said to read Acts 10:38 "...*God anointed Jesus of Nazareth with the Holy Ghost and with power: who went about doing good, and healing all that were oppressed of the devil for God was with him.*" He assured me that as a believer I could not be demon-possessed; however, I had been oppressed by this spirit of fear and was now free of that oppression. I was very happy to be free, but I was shocked–not by my deliverance, but that he took my money!

From that point on, I saw such a change in my thinking. I hadn't realized how preoccupied I had been because of this spirit of fear. I was now able to realize that my thoughts had been tormented for years. During that time of oppression, though, I assumed my fearful thought pattern was normal. After that night, my thinking was transformed. A new mole no longer meant skin cancer and constipation didn't mean colon cancer, etc. I was free in my mind just in time to discover there really was a serious problem in my body.

Bitten by the Serpent

Sharing it like this, it sounds as though the problem immediately followed the deliverance, but I'm not sure how much time passed before I discovered a lump in my left breast. The freedom from fear I had experienced was so blessed that my main concern after finding the lump was that the spirit of fear would return! I prayed for God's guidance and direction as to what I should do. Then I went to my husband and we prayed together.

Jesus said it isn't the well who need a physician but the sick, so I knew it would be fine for me to seek a doctor's care. However, even though I knew it wouldn't be wrong to go to a doctor, I felt impressed in my spirit to believe God. I didn't want to hear a bad report and allow fear to reenter my life. This became a spiritual battle for me. Before I go any further with my testimony, please understand that this is MY testimony. I don't want to imply that because this was God's direction for me at this time that it is also His direction for you. Each of us is led by God's Spirit in a very personal way. You need to do what He is telling *you* to do.

My husband and I agreed together in prayer that according to the

Word of God, Jesus took stripes for my healing and that healing was already accomplished. I wrote down several healing Scriptures and promises, and everyday I put these promises in my heart as I repeated them. The lump continued to grow, and I continued to stand fast in the Lord and in the power of His might. I knew that Satan comes to rob, kill, and destroy. He wanted to rob me of my deliverance, he wanted to destroy my faith, and he wanted to kill me. Jesus said that *He* had come to bring me life and that abundantly.

It's hard to have abundant life when you are in pain, but even though I had some physical discomfort, I didn't have any tormenting fears. I stood and trusted, but this seemed to have no effect on the lump. I wondered why my healing wasn't being manifested. I don't want to share with you how long I stood or all that I did in my faith fight, but I will tell you that my healing was detained. Do you know why? It was because I had a gap in the hedge. I had been bitten by the serpent and did not immediately realize this.

My daughter Mimi came to me one day and began to cry. She wanted me to see a doctor, she wanted me to be at her wedding, and she wanted me to live a long life, rejoicing in the sight of future grandchildren. As she cried, I cried, and I finally agreed that it would be wise for me to make an appointment for a mammogram.

I followed through as I had promised her, and as soon as the x-ray was reviewed, I was told to remain. The doctor wanted to speak with me. He told me there was a large mass in my left breast and he wanted to schedule a biopsy. Could I return tomorrow?

Tomorrow! I felt like it was one more night with the frogs! Remember when Pharaoh asked Moses to pray for him during the plague of the frogs, and Moses came back to Pharaoh and said God was ready to deliver them? As a matter of fact, what Moses asked Pharaoh was on the order of "So, when do you want this plague removed?" "*Then Pharaoh called for Moses and Aaron, and said, Entreat the Lord, that he may take* *away the frogs from me, and from my people; and I will let the people go, that they may do sacrifice unto the L*ORD*. And Moses said unto Pharaoh... when shall I entreat for thee... and [Pharaoh] said TOMORROW"* (Exodus 8:8-10*a*, emphasis mine).

I had already planned a board meeting for that day with six of the women who help me in running the ministry, Proclaiming His Word. I found it difficult to concentrate on our agenda because of my inner fear and dread of the pending biopsy, but I thank God for my friends. They were able to minister to me that day when I told them of my concern over the results of my mammogram. Right away they wanted to pray over me. As Sister Shirley began to pray, a word from the Lord came to her: *"The curse causeless shall not come"* (Proverbs 26:2). She asked the Lord to show me why the curse had come and why my healing had been delayed.

I have to tell you that this seemed strange to me. For months and months I had been praying and I thought I was praying in faith, trusting Jesus and His word. But as soon as Shirley said, "Amen," the Holy Spirit spoke to my heart and convicted me that I was in sin. What sin? Although the Lord was rebuking me, I was clueless initially as to what I could have done. When His still, small voice spoke again, He said I hadn't been praying in faith but I was instead living in the sin of worry. I knew in an instant that I had never entered that rest of faith that is God's plan for us. Instead, I had been trying to do the works of faith from the flesh.

Much like Job, the thing I had greatly feared had come upon me. *"I was not in safety, neither had I rest, neither was I quiet; yet trouble came"* (Job 3:26). That very day I repented of the sin of worrying, and the moment I acknowledged my sin, He cleansed me and healed me. The mass actually disintegrated in my breast! I revisited the doctor, and he confirmed the improvement and canceled the biopsy; the next mammogram was absolutely clear and clean. Hallelujah! All of my checkups since then have been problem-free, but even better than that, I have been free from fear. I am always on guard for the subtle sin of worry.

Not only have I lived to see my daughter Mimi's wedding, but at the time of this writing, I also have a granddaughter who's almost five and a wonderful little grandson who is almost two years old. I will continue, through God's grace, to be on guard for anything that might put a gap in my hedge and allow Satan to bite me.

Repentance Closes the Gap

For me, the key was found in repentance. Job also repented and God restored to Job twice what he had earlier lost. The New Testament book of James tells us to consider the end of the book of Job and see how the Lord was tender, showing Job mercy.

> *So the Lord blessed the latter end of Job more than his beginning for he had fourteen thousand sheep, and six thousand camels, and a thousand yoke of oxen, and a thousand she asses. He also had seven sons and three daughters. And he called the name of the first, Jemima; and the name of the second, Kezia; and the name of the third, Kerenhappuch. And in all the land were no women found so fair as the daughters of Job; and their father gave them inheritance among their brethren* (Job 42:12-15).

Some people wonder why Job's wealth was restored twofold but he only had ten more children. In chapter one of Job we read that he originally had seven sons and three daughters. At the end of the book of Job he has another seven sons and three daughters. If Job's first set of children went to be with the Lord after their physical death, then Job still had twice as many children as he started with.

We serve a God who is concerned most about reconciliation and restoration. When we repent of the sin that separates us from God, restoration can come and we are no longer slaves to sin. Once Job repented of his sin, he was restored and his captivity was turned. While that is wonderful, even better is the fact that the gap was closed in his hedge, and though he had once been bitten by the serpent, the venom didn't continue to poison his life and the life of his family. How can we be sure of this? Let's look more closely at Job's "second family."

How would you like Kerenhappuch for your first name? Kezia and Jemima are not quite such unusual names, but what is rare is that all three of the girls are listed by name. There are many lists in the Old Testament of the names of sons born to the men of old, but not lists of daughters. Why this reversal in the book of Job? Let's look at what these girls' names actually mean.

Jemima is Job's first daughter, and her name means "dove." His second daughter is named Kezia, which means "healing flower." His third daughter has the unusual name of Kerenhappuch, but that name means "light." As is customary in the Old Testament times, these names actually recounted the history of the one who named them. You see, once the dove of God's spirit came, Job was healed, and he walked in the light.

Yes, when we repent and when we close the gap our sin has made in our hedge, not only will the Lord restore us, but He will see that—like Job's daughters—we receive an inheritance. It doesn't matter what gender we are, we need the dove, we need healing, and most of all, we need the light. Without light, we can't see the gaps, we're not aware of the battle, and we don't see how the enemy attacks us.

Let's not wait to be poisoned by the venom of the viper before we know we have a problem. Let's ask the Lord to search our hearts daily, convicting us of all sin, so that we may repent and be restored.

How About You?

1. Where do you think there might be a gap or a "weak link" in your hedge?

2. What can you do to close the gap and strengthen the hedge?

3. List some fears you have wrestled with. How did you overcome these fears?

4. Do a word study, using a concordance, on the word *worry*. Memorize three scriptures that you can meditate on or say out loud when you are tempted to worry.

Venom of the Viper

You may have seen the dark comedy *Arsenic and Old Lace* in which two sweet old ladies poison quite a few sad elderly men in order to end their misery. This story is so ridiculous that it is funny. However, in reality there is nothing sweet about being poisoned, and there is nothing funny about our real enemy who plans to destroy us. The enemy is not a dear old granny but the devil, often described in the Word as a serpent full of deadly poison.

"They shall be burnt with hunger, and devoured with burning heat, and with bitter destruction: I will also send the teeth of beasts upon them, with the poison of serpents of the dust" (Deuteronomy 32:24). The poison of serpents, huh? If we check back in Genesis 3 where the serpent was confined to crawl on his belly after the Fall, we see that part of the curse was that he would eat dust all the days of his life. This presents a real problem for all of us in that the Bible states God made us from the dust of the earth. So, who do you think is the devil's main course?

"Their poison is like the poison of the serpent, they are like the deaf adder that stoppeth her ear; which will not hearken to the voice of charmers, charming never so wisely" (Psalm 58:4,5). We need to find out what the poison of the serpent is and how it is administered so that we have some defensive strategy. Many of us would run from an actual snake–especially a snake we knew was poisonous. Satan knows that, too, so he tries to disguise himself so that we won't recognize our danger. He's not going around wearing a neon sign with a skull and crossbones. He's subtle and sly, and he's after the "dust of the earth." He wants to destroy us by getting us to give in to the gall of bitterness–that's the venom of the viper.

If I wanted to poison my husband, I certainly wouldn't walk up to him with a large glass of arsenic-laced lemonade that was labeled TOXIC, and say, "Honey, are you thirsty?" No, a much more successful method would be for me to slip him small amounts of poison in his meals. My poor husband wouldn't even know he was being poisoned, then, until the effects began to surface. The enemy knows that he will be more successful if he gradually wears us down by slipping in a few negative thoughts here, an insult or two there, and regular opportunities to take offense–especially when we're tired.

Let's look at Job again. We know Job was figuratively bitten by a serpent. *"Yet his meat in his bowels is turned, it is the gall of asps within him"* (Job 20:14). *"He shall suck the poison of asps: the viper's tongue shall slay him"* (Job 20:16). These verses equate the gall of asps with the poison and venom of the viper. Asp is an old English word for snake. The New International Version translates verse 14, *"Yet his food will turn sour in his stomach; it will become the venom of serpents within him.."* The word for venom is gall, and we know that gall is the poison of bitterness. Let me tell you that bitterness kills even more effectively than poison. *"And another dieth in bitterness of his soul, and never eateth with pleasure. They shall lie down alike in the dust"* (Job 21:25,26a). That doesn't sound like the way I want to go. We are made of dust, and to dust we will return; but I don't want to go out having been spiritually poisoned, dying a slow death of bitterness. Do you?

Lest you think I'm giving bitterness too much of a bad rap, check out these verses. *"For their vine is the vine of Sodom, and of the fields of Gomorrah: their grapes are grapes of gall, their clusters are bitter. Their wine is the poison of dragons, and the cruel venom of asps.* (Deuteronomy 32:32,33). Who are these people who are being chastised so severely? They are God's people who have become rebellious and disobedient, leaning on their own understanding and not acknowledging God as God. We see another such caution in Deuteronomy 29:18 *"Lest there should be among you man, or woman, or family, or tribe, whose heart turneth away this day from the Lord our God, to go and serve the gods of these nations; Lest there should be among you a root that beareth gall and wormwood."* The NIV translates this the last phrase, *"make sure there is no root among you that produces such bitter poison.."*

A Deadly Trap

The New Testament supplies us with warnings as well. *"Their throat is an open sepulcher; with their tongues they have used deceit; the poison of asps (coiling serpent) is under their lips: Whose mouth is full of cursing and bitterness"* (Romans 3:13,14). Who is Paul writing about? Those who do not fear God; or in other words, those who don't consider it important to obey Him. Could this ever apply to believers? Unfortunately, yes. *"But the tongue can no man tame; it is an unruly evil, full of deadly poison... Out of the same mouth proceed blessing and cursing. My brethren, these things ought not so to be. Doth a fountain send forth at the same place sweet water and bitter?"* (James 3:8,10,11). James is definitely speaking to believers. Read what he says a few verses later. *"Who is a wise man and endued with knowledge among you? let him shew out of a good conversation his works with meekness of wisdom. But if ye have bitter envying and strife in your hearts, glory not, and lie not against the truth...For where envying and strife is, there is confusion and every evil work"* (James 3:13,14,16). Hmmm. Buying into the enemy's arguments through the poison of bitterness is a horribly dangerous mistake.

Numbers 21 tells the story of the people of God as they journeyed from Mount Hor to the land of Edom. The people became discouraged, and once again they began to speak against Moses and against God, complaining and grumbling. They said that their souls loathed the light bread (not the 40-calorie diet variety, but the manna God was providing for them on their travels). What happened next was a manifestation in the natural or physical world of what was really happening in the spiritual realm. The Bible says that God sent fiery serpents among the people, and as they were bitten by the snakes, those bitten died. The people quickly began to repent. (I guess I'd repent pretty quickly, too, if I saw people dying all around me and snakes everywhere.) They acknowledged their sin against Moses and against God.

> *Therefore the people came to Moses, and said, We have sinned, for we have spoken against the LORD and against thee; pray unto the LORD, that he take away the serpents from us. And Moses prayed for the people. And the LORD said unto Moses, Make thee a fiery serpent, and set it upon a pole: and it shall come to pass, that everyone that is bitten, when he looketh upon it, shall live (Numbers 21: 7,8).*

Please note that another word for fiery is burning. When we are bitten by the serpent, there will be a time of burning. In the case of the deliverance God sent, the burning wasn't from the devil but from God. The Bible tells us our God is a consuming fire. (See Deuteronomy 4:24). There will always be a burning when we get into sin. Remember it was God who sent this punishment to His children.

We must always examine ourselves before we assume that every problem or punishment is from the devil. The Hebrew people were bitten because they murmured against Moses, complaining about what God had provided. It wasn't the first time they complained, and it wouldn't be the last. In fact, members of Moses' own family were not exempt either from criticizing him or being punished for their bitter words. This is a good example for us to take to heart because so many times it is those who are closest to us who can come against us. If we are not careful to let go of the hurt, the resentment, and the anger, then we open ourselves up to have some fiery serpents snack on us.

Problems in a Biblical Family

The time that Moses' family spoke out against him is found in Numbers in the twelfth chapter. Miriam and Aaron didn't like the wife Moses had chosen because she was an Ethiopian woman. Women from Ethiopia are dark skinned. I don't want to say that the only struggle here was one of racism because some other resentments are expressed in the next verse. *"And they said Hath the LORD indeed spoken only by Moses? hath he not spoken also by us? And the LORD heard it"* (Numbers 12:2). They had an issue against Moses' wife because of racism, but in verse two they also express pride and spiritual jealousy. Not good.

So how did God deal with Miriam and Aaron? They were in what we might consider the inner circle or the elite, but they were not exempt from discipline. God is not a respecter of persons. God was so angry with them that He came down in a pillar of the cloud and stood in the door of the tabernacle and called to Aaron and Miriam. When the cloud lifted, Miriam was leprous. Whew! That was a terrible death sentence and an obvious mark of sin. But why did God only put the leprosy on her and not on her brother Aaron? They were both guilty of speaking against Moses and his wife. At the start of the chapter, Miriam is named first, but when God calls them, He names Aaron first.

Miriam started this complaining and involved her brother Aaron. He seems easily influenced by those around him. Remember the incident of the golden calf? The people wanted Aaron to make them a golden god when Moses was busy on the mountain talking to the real God. Aaron did just what the people wanted even though he knew it was wrong. *"And the people brake off the golden earrings which were in their ears, and brought them to Aaron. And he received them at their hand, and fashioned it with a graving tool, after he had made it a molten calf: and they said, These be thy gods, O Israel, which brought thee up out of the land of Egypt"* (Exodus 32:3,4).[1]

When Moses came down from the mountain of God, he was appalled to see the people worshiping a golden calf, and he began questioning his brother, Aaron. Aaron began to shift the blame to the people and made one of the lamest excuses you could ever hear. *"And I said unto them, Whosoever hath any gold, let them break it off. So they gave it me: then I cast it into the fire, and there came out this calf"* (Exodus 32:24). What did he mean out came this calf? Yeah, right. Like the gold shaped and molded itself in the fire and out jumped an idol.

Later, even if Aaron was influenced by his sister, he was still a partner in this sin of rebellion. He asked Moses, *"Lay not the sin upon us, wherin we have done foolishly, and wherein we have sinned"* (Numbers 12:11*b*). Sounds like an admission of guilt to me. Since Miriam got the leprosy, though, and he didn't, what's the deal? For years I never understood why he didn't get the same judgment she did. We know from the Bible that leprosy made the person who had it unclean and that it represents sin. What I didn't realize was that the reason Aaron wasn't smitten with leprosy is that anyone who was unclean could not go before the Lord.

The Lord had told Aaron that no one from among his seed could enter into the presence of God if he had any blemish. He could not approach the altar and offer the shewbread of God. So if Aaron had received the same visible punishment as his sister Miriam, we wouldn't have a line of priests. He was the first high priest, remember? If he had been defiled, the whole line of the priesthood would have been defiled and kept outside of God's presence.

We are all unclean whether we have leprosy on the outside or not. We need to be cleansed from within. The Word says, *"For all have sinned, and come short of the glory of God"* (Romans 3:23), but it also says that Jesus came as our high priest to cleanse us and open the way into God's presence for us.

It's kind of a shock to realize that God put leprosy on Miriam. Thank God that when Aaron and Miriam both repented of their sin, Moses prayed for them and the Lord healed Miriam. Still, it was a great price to pay for sin. Look at the effect of their disobedience, the same effect we are subject to. First, Miriam became unclean. Second, her uncleanness resulted in broken fellowship—she had to stay outside the camp. Third, the whole experience hindered the progress of all the children of Israel. Disobedience gives the devil access to us, and it also produces the need for chastisement from God and cleansing. Serpents, leprosy, and lions were used to alert people to the seriousness of their sin. We don't need to live in fear of them, though, if we will just fear the Lord and obey Him.

Let's go back to our opening story in Numbers 21. The people in this story asked Moses to intercede for them just as Aaron did in Numbers 12. Remember that God instructed Moses to do something very peculiar. He was told to make a fiery serpent and set it upon a pole. When anyone was bitten, if they just looked at the serpent on the pole they would live. So Moses made a serpent of brass (or in some versions, bronze). Both brass and bronze represent judgment and Jesus quoted this event in the gospel of Saint John.

"Ye Must Be Born Again!"

When a Pharisee by the name of Nicodemus came to Jesus by night, he said, *"Rabbi, we know that thou art a teacher come from God: for no man can do these miracles that thou doest, except God be with him"* (John 3:2b). Jesus responds to Nicodemus that unless a man is born again, he will not see the kingdom of God. Nicodemus asked the same question you or I would have asked, *"How can that be "How can a man be born when he is old? can he enter the second time into his mother's womb, and be born?"* (Let me just say as a mother of two, the answer is "No!" It was all I could do to get my children out, and even the thought of them wanting to reenter gives me nightmares.)

Jesus told Nicodemus that except a man be born of water and of the spirit, he cannot enter into the kingdom of God. Nicodemus still didn't understand what Jesus meant, so the Lord went on to tell him that the things He was speaking of concerned the spirit. He began to talk about the wind and the Spirit of God. He then said, *"And no man hath ascended up to heaven, but he that came down from heaven, even the Son of man which is in heaven. And as Moses lifted up the serpent in the wilderness, even so must the Son of man be lifted up: That whosoever believeth in him should not perish, but have eternal life"* (John 3:13-15).

Since Satan is the god of this world, all of us who are born in this world are under his spiritual control, prior to our salvation. There are many who may not even be aware of this. John wrote, *"We know [positively] that we are of God, and the whole world [around us] is under the power of the evil one"* (1 John 5:19, Amplified Bible). There were other Jews, besides Nicodemus, who came to Jesus and called themselves children of Abraham. Jesus stunned them when He told them that they were of their father the devil. So, how do we change our fatherhood? If the devil is the father of the natural, sinful man, then that which is natural must become spiritual.

Stick with me and we'll see how this can happen. God told Adam in the Garden that the day he ate of the tree of the knowledge of good and evil, he would die. God never lies and yet didn't Adam and Eve live for years and years after their act of disobedience? What happened? It was not their physical bodies but their spirits which died at the moment of sin. Before sinning, they had been alive to a close fellowship with God. They walked and talked with him in the cool of the day. After they sinned and they died, they were separated from God, hiding from His presence. They, like so many of us, didn't recognize the real enemy. God wasn't their enemy and yet they were afraid of Him and hid.

God sent Jesus to restore what Adam had lost. Hallelujah! As a matter of fact, in 1 Corinthians 15, Jesus is called the last Adam. When we turn from sin and receive Jesus, our spirits–formerly dead in sin–quicken and are alive before God. Thus we receive eternal life. Let me continue to clear up another important issue. Christians use the term eternal life, but isn't everyone an eternal being? Some will live in eternal torment and others in eternal paradise, so what's the issue with eternal life. *"And this is life eternal, that they might know thee [the Father] the only true God and Jesus Christ, whom thou hast sent"* (John 17:3). Did you see that phrasing?

Not just eternal life, but Life Eternal. Yes, all people live forever, but without salvation and being born again, even though they live eternally, it will not be life eternal in the kingdom of God. "*But as many as received him, to them gave he power to become the sons of God, even to them that believe on his name*" (John 1:12). So once we receive Jesus as Savior and Lord, we are translated from the kingdom of Satan to the kingdom of God. We are no longer sons of the devil, but adopted sons into the family of God.

Back to Nicodemus. He was told by Jesus that as Moses lifted up the serpent, so would Jesus also be lifted up and that whosoever looked to Him would live–just as those who looked to the bronze serpent lived and were healed of the venom of the viper. As we look to the cross, we also will live.

He who knew no sin, became sin for us. Jesus bore our sins on the cross, and sin originated with the serpent. To have Moses display a serpent on the pole that was lifted up showed the judgment of God for sin and the works of Satan. Jesus said in John 14:30*b*, "*The prince of this world cometh, and hath nothing in me.*" Remember what the serpents in the wilderness put into the children of God? They were poisoned by the venom of the viper.

Defeating the Serpent
The venom is the gall of bitterness. Remember, when Jesus was lifted up on the cross, He was offered gall. This was prophesied much earlier. "*They gave me also gall for my meat; and in my thirst they gave me vinegar to drink*" (Psalm 69:21). Read Matthew 27:33,34. "*And when they were come unto a place called Golgotha, that is to say, a place of a skull, They gave him vinegar to drink mingled with gall: and when he had tasted thereof, he would not drink.*" Thank You, Jesus, that You willingly went to the cross and that even on the cross You didn't have any bitterness. You refused to drink the gall. Instead of the serpent poisoning You, You defeated him for us.

Jesus was offered three things on the cross: myrrh, gall, and vinegar. Jesus refused the gall, He wasn't bitter at the assignment of God, and He was not and is not bitter with us. Only He can remove the bitter poison that the enemy has put into our lives. Jesus didn't carry any personal bitterness, and that's the reason He is able to deliver us from our bitterness. This is wonderful good news!

What about the myrrh? He didn't drink the myrrh either. Why not? Wasn't it one of the first gifts He received as a child when the wise men came to Him? Think of the gifts they gave Him. Gold was the gift given to a king, frankincense was a gift that signified His priesthood, and myrrh was a gift for burial. Jesus, the King of kings and the Lord of lords became a man in order to become our High Priest. The only way He could do this was to die. The significance of the presents is clear.

Since He had already received the myrrh as a baby, and He rejected the gall, what was left was the vinegar. This He received on the cross, according to the gospel of John. When Jesus said, *"I thirst,"* someone soaked a sponge in wine vinegar, put it upon a stick of hyssop, and Jesus drank of it. The significance seems to lie more in the hyssop than in the vinegar.

The first time we are introduced to hyssop is in Exodus when the lambs were killed and their blood was applied to the doors of the homes of the children of God. This was to save them from the plague of the firstborn dying in Egypt. The blood was to be applied with a hyssop plant. The last time we see hyssop is when the Lamb of God dies on the cross. Only this time it was God's firstborn, His beloved Son.

The only way we will recover from the gall and bitterness in our lives, when we have been bitten by the serpent, is to look to the cross. Jesus destroyed the works of the devil, and He can remove the poison from our hearts and the gall we have swallowed. Some of us have been poisoned by bitterness and gall for years, but it's not too late to look up and live. Calvary is the antidote for the venom of the viper.

Victory over Snakebite

There is another story in the Bible about a man of God being bitten

110

by a snake. He wasn't bitten because of any disobedience; we don't see any gap in his hedge; and the way he treated this viper is a lesson for us all.

Paul had just survived a shipwreck. He landed on the island of Malta and was cold and tired. The people there had prepared a fire to dry him and warm him.

> *And when Paul had gathered a bundle of sticks, and laid them on the fire, there came a viper out of the heat, and fastened on his hand. And when the barbarians saw the venomous beast hang on his hand they said among themselves, No doubt this man is a murderer, whom, though he hath escaped the sea, yet vengeance suffereth not to live. And he shook off the beast into the fire and felt no harm. Howbeit they looked when he should have swollen, or fallen down dead suddenly; but after they had looked a great while, and saw no harm come to him, they changed their minds, and said that he was a god.* (Acts 28:3-6).

The venomous viper should have killed the Apostle Paul in the natural realm, yet he doesn't swell nor does he fall over dead. The reason is twofold. Number one, he shook it off: we don't see any fear in him or any panic; he simply shook it off. Number two, he shook it off into the fire. Read what the Word says about Jesus' victory. "*Blotting out the handwriting of ordinances that was against us, which was contrary to us, and took it out of the way, nailing it to his cross; And having spoiled principalities and powers, he made a shew of them openly, triumphing over them in it*" (Colossians 2:14,15). Part of this victory and triumph is displayed as Jesus gives us power as well. "*Behold, I give unto you power to tread on serpents and scorpions, and over all the power of the enemy: and nothing shall by any means hurt you*" (Luke 10:19). Even as He ascended into heaven, He gave the disciples the Great Commission of going into all the world and preaching the gospel to every creature. "*He that believeth and is baptized shall be saved; but he that believeth not shall be damned*" (Mark 16:16). We usually stop quoting there, but Jesus went on to say something that is of vital importance to anyone who's been bitten or poisoned.

And these signs shall follow them that believe; In my name shall they cast out devils; they shall speak with new tongues; They shall take up serpents; and if they drink any deadly thing, it shall not hurt them; they shall lay hands on the sick, and they shall recover (Mark 16:17,18).

I don't think the Lord meant for us to handle physical snakes, although this promise held good in the natural for Paul. We're not to drink the venom of serpents to show the world His power is in us. I believe that the deadly thing wanting to harm us is the venom of the viper, which is the gall of bitterness.

Let's go back to Paul, who said, "Follow me, as I follow Christ." Yes, let's follow him, and when the venomous viper fastens to our hands or our hearts, let's shake him off–into the fire of God. We should also imitate Paul in the most important thing he did: he moved right on into ministry. The people on the island of Malta began to tell others the story of the viper and the fact that Paul lived. It wasn't long before Paul laid hands on a man who was sick with fever and healed him. Soon, the people were bringing everyone on the Island who was sick, and God through Paul healed them all.

Delivered to Serve

After we shake the viper into God's fire, we must move on with ministry. Joseph, one of Jacob's twelve sons is an excellent example of this. He overcame the temptation to harbor great bitterness. Betrayed by his own family members, sold into slavery, Joseph was then thrown into prison. In his innocence, the Word of God says of Joseph over and over again, "God was with him," and God made him to prosper. In the Psalms we read that the word of the Lord tried Joseph. I believe he passed the test by not allowing himself to be bitter with his family, his circumstances, or even his God.

From the pit to the palace–in a moment's time Joseph is delivered and elevated to a place of authority. After his amazing promotion, Joseph marries and the testimony of his heart is found in Genesis 41 in the record of the birth of his two sons. *"And Joseph called the name of the firstborn Manasseh: For God, said he, hath made me forget all my toil, and all my father's house. And the name of the second called he Ephraim: For God hath caused me to be fruitful in the land of my affliction"* (verse 51).

I don't want any more children. I was blessed with a daughter and a son, and I now have some grandchildren. However, in one sense, there are two children I need to have. These are spiritual children: a Manasseh and an Ephraim. We all need to birth these children out of our spirits. Manasseh–for God has caused me to forget. Oh, how badly we all need to forget the pain of our past: the bitterness, the disappointments, the failures. Once we have done that, we need to birth an Ephraim–God has made me fruitful in the land of affliction.

Shake off the bitterness, look to the Lord Jesus for healing, and be available for the ministry He has planned for you. Put your hand to the next thing the Spirit is speaking to you, whether it's repentance or teaching a Sunday School class. It may take some time, but one day you will find that your obedience to Him has caused you to bear much fruit for His kingdom and has made glad the heart of God.

How About You?

1. Have you ever been to a zoo and visited the reptile house? How careful do the handlers of the venomous snakes have to be? If the cages were to open, how fast would you flee? Can you apply the same caution in the spirit that you would exercise in the flesh?

2. Why do you think God's Word represents Satan as a serpent? (You may want to do a word study on this, going back to Genesis.)

3. Jesus also called the Pharisees vipers. Read Matthew 23 and see where the poison comes into this situation. This is a hard question, but are there areas in your life where you may be operating as a Pharisee? Ask the Holy Spirit to identify attitudes that are not godly ones, and repent of them.

4. How can you build up an immunity to the poison of the serpent? Rather than taking it in small doses, we need to reach for the antidote of God's Word right away. Which verses will you memorize so that you are prepared for the moment of temptation?

End Notes

1. For a fascinating teaching that explains the significance of the gold earrings, read Judson Cornwall's book, *Things We Adore.*

Chapter 8

Good Grief

Here we go with another oxymoron: good grief. Is there ever a time that grief is good? Aren't sorrow and loss things we want to avoid? I have counseled and prayed for many people over the years, and I have discovered that the loss of a loved one is a prime time for hidden bitterness to develop. Each of us will experience loss of one kind or another; it's a part of being human. But what we don't have to experience are the negative thoughts and the blame, the accusations, regrets, and hurt that lead to bitterness.

In the first chapter we took a short look at a woman in the Bible who experienced grave bitterness. She was bitter about the death of her loved ones, and she blamed God. Many of us have also been bitter with the Lord. Oh, we don't express it out loud, necessarily, but as we try to hide our feelings and swallow the pain, the poison of bitterness begins to pollute our lives. When disappointment or disillusion with others creeps in, there is a tendency for us as Christians to bury our feelings because what would others think if they knew we were bitter with God Himself? Saddest of all are those who are in such denial they don't even admit to themselves that they are angry with God. It's very hard to receive healing when we don't confess a need for it.

Come with me to the land of Bethlehem-Judah. *Bethlehem* means "house of bread" and *Judah* means "praise."[1] During the time we are examining, a famine had come to the land of Bethlehem-Judah; and instead of praising, trusting, and waiting for God's direction, a man named Elimelech took his wife and their sons to the land of Moab. You can find this story in chapter one of the book of Ruth. We discover that Moab was actually the land of the enemy. In Ruth 1:1, we are told Elimelech sojourned in the country of Moab, in verse 2 we are told he continued there, and by verse 4, he had lived there ten years.

Elimelech reminds me of Lot. In Genesis we read that Lot, Abraham's nephew, pitched his tent toward Sodom. Before much longer, he is dwelling in Sodom, and finally, he is seated at the gate of Sodom—indicating he has some sort of governmental position there. Both Lot and Elimelech were out of the will of God to look for substance and provision from the hands of God's enemies and not to seek God Himself for provision.

The book of Ruth spends very little time describing those ten years that Elimelech, his wife, Naomi, and his two sons, Mahlon and Chilion, lived in Moab because the next statement is that Elimelech died. How tragic for Naomi to be in a foreign country and lose her husband! The name *Naomi* means "pleasant and joyful," but I doubt that she felt that way at this time. She became a single mom, but her difficulties didn't stop there. Her two sons also had descriptive names: *Mahlon* means "sickly" and *Chilion* means "wasting away." It seems reasonable to assume that maybe they weren't in the best of health.

Naomi's sons lived long enough to marry pagan wives—a thing that was strictly forbidden by Jewish law. Can you see some gaps in the hedge here? They are in a land God did not send them to and are now joined to what the Bible calls "strange women." (See 1 Kings 11:1,2). The daughters of the Moabites were not even allowed in the house of God (Deuteronomy 23:3); and the next thing we know about this family is that both of Naomi's sons die.

The Pain of Grief

How many widows are there in the church, who after burying their husbands find themselves also burying their bitterness toward the Lord? I'm not saying that every woman is bitter who is grieving the loss of her mate, but I have seen that this is a prime time for the enemy to attack with the temptation to become bitter. Those women who are also attempting the difficult task of raising children alone may have to deal with much hurt and resentment.

Naomi hears that the Lord is blessing His people in the land of Judah, and with a heavy heart she determines to return to her homeland. One of her daughters-in-law, Ruth, insists on going with Naomi.

> *So they two went until they came to Bethlehem. And it came to pass, when they were come to Bethlehem, that all the city was moved about them, and they said Is this Naomi? And she said unto them, Call me not Naomi, call me Mara: for the Almighty hath dealt very bitterly with me. I went out full, and the Lord hath brought me home again empty: why then call ye me Naomi, seeing the Lord hath testified against me, and the Almighty hath afflicted me?* (Ruth 1:19-21)

Had the Lord really afflicted her? The word *afflict* means "to break in pieces, to be good for nothing."[2] Naomi, this once pleasant, joyful woman, now wants to be called *Mara*, which, of course, means bitterness. Naomi could only see and feel her pain, and it seems to me that if the townspeople had to ask if this were really Naomi, she must not even have looked like her old self. When we have suffered loss and death and disappointment, the wear and tear will eventually show in our countenance.

Although Naomi may have felt broken and good for nothing, the Lord had good plans for her. He didn't want her to be good for nothing. When we are in the middle of the pain of grief, we live in the past and have little hope for our future. But God doesn't give up so easily. In the midst of our pain and bitterness, He is still at work. We have seen Naomi's beginning; now let's look at her ending.

> *And the women said unto Naomi, Blessed be the Lord, which hath not left thee this day without a kinsman, that his name may be famous in Israel. And he shall be unto thee a restorer of thy life and a nourisher of thine old age: for thy daughter in law, which loveth thee, which is better to thee than seven sons, hath borne him* (Ruth 4:14,15)

This represents quite a change. What happened to bring about such a glorious conclusion? Who is this famous relative? Before we answer these questions, let's see what this verse says about Naomi and her Lord. "*Blessed be the Lord, which has not left thee this day...*" Not only didn't He leave her that day, He had been with her all of her days through her hurts, her pain, her sorrow, her grief, and even her bitterness towards Him. "*And he shall be to thee a restorer of thy life.*" Once we have experienced the death of a loved one, we need our lives restored, and we need hope and help. The verse goes on to say that she will be nourished in her old age and that she is loved. You see, her daughter-in-law, Ruth, is about to give birth to Obed, who will be the father of Jesse, who will be the father of King David.

When We Suffer Grief upon Grief

When we are in grief, we need to hold on to the future that God has prepared for us. This takes faith, but He will supply all we need. He will never leave us nor forsake us. He has a future and a hope to do us good. There was a time in my own life when no one could have called me pleasant or joyful, but I can testify that the Lord has restored me and He has nourished me—and even though I don't have any famous great-great grandchildren yet, who knows?

I can relate a little to Naomi. She suffered the loss of her loved ones almost back to back. We don't know the exact time span between the death of her husband and the death of her children, but it doesn't seem very long. What we are sure of is that she suffered greatly.

On Mother's Day in 1978, my father suffered a devastating stroke. He was left totally paralyzed on his right side, and he lost his ability to speak. The hardest part of his handicap was that he couldn't communicate with us. Several months into his therapy, my mother went for a physical only to find out that she had terminal cancer. My parents had only been Christians for a few years, and during that time they had become happy, healthy, and fun-loving. Within a few months, they became like Mahlon and Chilion, sickly and wasting away. My mother's condition deteriorated very quickly once the diagnosis was made. In just a few short months, she was bedridden, and my dad would sit in his wheelchair right by her bed and cry. While this was very difficult for me to bear, even worse was the heartache and pain that would follow. You see, several things happened before their death that wounded me greatly—mostly due to things other Christians had done. Surely the enemy had moved me into a famine. During the next couple of years, I allowed much bitterness to come into my heart toward God and His people.

I find it very sad to say that in all the years I have been serving Jesus, the world has caused me little pain. Oh, I've experienced persecution and rejection at times from the world, but it's been mild in comparison to what the Body of Christ has inflicted. The first deep hurt came from one of my closest sisters in the Lord. During my parents' illness, we had decided to keep Mom at her home. We didn't have the Hospice program to help us at that time, and it was very stressful trying to care for my parents and my own family. My children were eight and nine years old at this time, so they needed quite a bit of care themselves. Managing two households proved to be very taxing.

I was able to find a woman to come in for four hours twice a week, which gave me time to attend to my own household. Otherwise, I practically lived at my folks' home. I had also been involved with a women's ministry that held weekly prayer meetings at one the ladies' homes. One afternoon I felt that I really needed to be with the Lord's people. I wanted fellowship and I wanted prayer. So I went to this prayer meeting where there were about a dozen women in attendance. I was so happy to be there and I was in such need. After a time of praise and worship, we gathered in a circle to pray. One of the women began speaking what I thought initially was a word from the Lord.

The prophecy turned into a personal word directed at me. She said, "I, the Lord, have afflicted your mother and your father to see if you love Me." She said several more things after that, but my mind couldn't take them in. I felt as if someone had thrust a knife into my heart. What could the Lord mean? I didn't love Him enough and therefore my parents would suffer for my lack of love? I do remember the ending of her so-called word from the Lord, that I was to remember Lazarus. I stood there in shock, waiting for one of the other women, who were more mature in the Lord, to say something. No one did.

I left the prayer meeting, assuming that the Lord had spoken this word to me. What could I do to show God I really loved Him? This question burned in my heart every day and sometimes every hour. Other questions arose. If I read more of my Bible or prayed longer, if I fasted or gave my food to the Lord, would He then know that I loved Him? I kept asking Him what I should do to prove my love so that He wouldn't kill my parents.

My mother died in July at the age of 59, and only six weeks later, my father died in my arms. I really wasn't prepared for their deaths. I knew they were saved and therefore were with the Lord, but I felt I needed them more than He did. The Word says we are not to grieve as those who have no hope. I knew we would be reunited at the resurrection, but that seemed such a long way off. I recall days when I would go food shopping, and as I walked up and down each aisle I looked in the faces of strangers, wondering does life just go on? I felt like an orphan, lost and alone in my sorrow and pain.

The words of this sister had deeply affected me, causing me to think that perhaps I had played a part in their deaths. I was filled with bitterness towards this sister, but would not admit to feeling more than hurt and anger. It was because I harbored unforgiveness toward her, though, that bitterness entered my heart. I tried to avoid this woman, but it seemed almost as if she had become my shadow. If I were invited to speak at a ladies' luncheon, she would be the guest soloist. Wasn't there anywhere I could go to be rid of her? If I didn't see her, maybe I could forget what she had said.

Testing the Word

My doubts were compounded because I felt so alone. There were certainly times when I thought her "word from the Lord" had been spoken out of turn, but if that was so, why didn't one of the other sisters say something. The Bible tells us we are to judge prophecies (1 Corinthians 14:29), but no one did or said anything to judge this word. After months of turmoil, I pleaded with God to heal me of this wound, or somehow keep me out of this woman's way. It was then that the answer came from God. I was led by the Spirit first to Ezekiel 13:1-3. *"And the word of the Lord came unto me, saying, 'Son of man, prophesy against the prophets of Israel that prophesy, and say thou unto them that prophesy out of their own hearts, "Hear ye the word of the Lord; Thus saith the Lord God; Woe unto the foolish prophets, that follow their own spirit, and have seen nothing!"'"*

Next, I was directed to study Jeremiah 14:14. *"Then the Lord said unto me, 'The prophets prophesy lies in my name: I sent them not, neither have I commanded them, neither spake unto them: they prophesy unto you a false vision and divination, and a thing of nought, and the deceit of their heart.'"*

Finally, I was free from this false word. The woman is not a false prophet, but this particular word was false. You can have a right word from a wrong spirit–just look at Acts 16:16-18. You can also have a wrong word from a person with the right spirit. The reason we are told to judge prophecy is that when the word of the Lord comes, it comes through people. Whenever the flesh is involved, there is opportunity for human error. If spoken prophecy was always just from God alone, how dare we judge!

My Christian sister thought that this pain was a punishment from God due to some hidden sin or lack of love on my part. She spoke out of her human spirit, her own heart deceiving her. (Does this remind you of Job's counselors?) The part about remembering Lazarus was certainly wishful thinking since neither she nor the Lord raised them from the dead.

How can we know if a word that is spoken is indeed from the Lord? *"When a prophet speaketh in the name of the Lord, if the thing follow not, nor come to pass, that is the thing which the Lord hath not spoken, but the prophet hath spoken it presumptuously: thou shalt not be afraid of him"* (Deuteronomy 18:22). If only I had been able to discern the spirit in which this word was spoken, I would have been able to judge the word and save myself months of pain. At that time, I was too new a Christian to understand either what discernment was or how to apply it. This was to prove my downfall yet again.

The Need for Discernment
I was saved in a Methodist church where my parents had also become members. During the time of their illness, I attended a Wednesday night service where a guest speaker, a minister from Texas, gave the message. Toward the end of the service, he opened the altar for people to come and pray. I had a very heavy heart due to the suffering of both my parents, so I went forward and knelt at the altar, along with many others. What happened next really startled me. The guest minister walked over to me, bent down, and said, "I see someone with cancer, someone close to you, and the Lord is going to heal them." I burst into tears upon hearing this.

It seemed so supernatural. How could a minister from Texas know my mother's condition? Amid sobs, I told him it was my mother who had cancer. By then my husband had joined me at the altar. We were convinced this was a word from the Lord and that Mom was going to be healed. Some friends agreed to take our children home so that we could go over to Mom's house to pray with her.

During the entire drive to Atlantic City where Mom lived, my husband, Boo, and I were praising and glorifying God. Wow! A minister all the way from Texas, singling me out of an altar full of people with this message! My Mom would surely be healed. We could hardly wait to get there to lay hands on her and pray for her to be well.

When we arrived, Mom was asleep, and my sister-in-law, Rosie, was there, tending to my parents. We woke Mom and told her what happened at church. Boo and I prayed in agreement with one another, and he anointed her with oil, as per the Scriptures. (Read James 5:13-18 if this is an unfamiliar concept to you.) We expected her to get up out of bed, fully healed. When she tried and just couldn't get up, we were stunned. What could have happened?

I was thrown into more disappointment, more despair, and more discouragement. I couldn't understand. Jesus healed people in the Bible; God's Word says He is the same yesterday, today, and forever, so why didn't He heal my mother? After my mom's death, I went to see my pastor. I needed some clarity on all of this. Wasn't this man given a "word of knowledge" for me, seeing that I was a stranger to him?

My pastor clarified the issue all right. He informed me that before the service that Wednesday evening, he had pointed me out to the guest speaker. He did so in innocence, sharing the concerns he had for my family in our difficult time. The guest minister then sinned against me by acting as though this had been a divine revelation to him. The damage he did took years to remove as my trust level dropped drastically. I hardened my heart against things of the spirit. First, the false prophecy from a friend, and then a false word of knowledge. I became very critical and overly cautious in reaction.

Since this is a book on bitterness and not one on healing, I can't deal with the deep subject of why my mom and dad weren't healed. I can tell you this, though. God has answered my questions. Over five years I studied daily the subject of healing—but I was not able to hear the answers or have fruitful study until I was able to admit my resentment and bitterness over these two events in my life. Please hear my heart on this. Bitterness and resentment will shut you into a prison where even your most desperate questions and prayers seem to fall on deaf ears. This is far worse than any physical condition could be.

Working through the Pain

Shortly after the death of both of my parents, I was to suffer one more wound at the hands of well-meaning Christians. I went away for the weekend to a retreat. I wasn't the speaker, and I traveled there with hopes of receiving ministry. You can imagine how relieved I was to find that one of the Saturday workshops was on grief, loss, and death. I didn't even have to pray. I knew for certain that this was the class for me to attend.

The woman who was teaching and facilitating this workshop had lost her own daughter to leukemia, and the workshop was truly anointed. I had all I could do to hold onto my composure. I sat in the class, feeling like a lost little girl. I so wanted my mommy and daddy to be back, but I knew that no matter how hard I looked, I would not be able to find them. Although I knew in my spirit that they were with the Lord, I surely missed them being with me.

Toward the end of the session, my grief and pain surfaced to the point where I couldn't hold back the sobs. For so many months I had had to be strong, first for my dad, then for my mom, and then for my unsaved family when Dad died. I was worn out physically and mentally. As I wept and sobbed, the announcement was made that it was time for lunch.

People began to file past me on their way to the cafeteria. Didn't anyone care about my pain? The speaker approached and told me to pull myself together and then join the others for lunch. Pulling myself together felt like an impossible instruction. I was falling apart in every direction, shattered and broken. I wanted to be obedient, though, so like a zombie, I rose and followed.

When we walked into the cafeteria, I had such a lump in my throat that I couldn't even conceive of eating anything. I told the two friends who had accompanied me to go ahead and have lunch without me. I needed to be alone with the Lord. They understood.

I walked back to my cabin, closed the door, and fell to my knees by my bunk. I don't recommend you do what I did that day. I started to yell and scream and cry, pressing my face into my pillow because if anyone heard me, they would have either put me out of the camp or put me away! So much pain, hurt, and bitterness came pouring out of me that afternoon, but the Lord did speak to me. I heard a Scripture reference within my heart, but I was afraid to trust it or even look it up in the Bible.

Hearing from God was not an entirely new concept to me. I had listened to a tape on this very topic just a few months before this retreat. I had listened to it three or four times and so was familiar with the principles recommended for hearing God's voice. The instructions included binding the enemy from speaking to you, praying to God, and listening. (That's actually an extremely short synopsis of a 90-minute teaching tape.) The speaker also recommended you should be alone, be reverent, and wait.

Well, I had tried this shortly after receiving the tape. I prepared my heart, played the tape one more time, and knelt by my bed. I took authority over the enemy, applied the blood, and asked the Lord to speak to me. Almost instantly I heard in my heart the reference Romans 18:8. Very excited, I jumped up, flew downstairs to get my Bible, and praised God with every step: *Oh thank you, Jesus, I hear the voice of the Good Shepherd.* I picked up my Bible, absolutely filled with expectation and anticipation for what the Lord would reveal to me.

You can imagine how disappointed I was to find that there are only sixteen chapters in the book of Romans. What had I done wrong? I realized that in my endeavor to hear from the Lord, I had overlooked the human spirit. I had bound the evil spirits, and I listened for the Holy Spirit—that much was right—but I somehow forgot my human spirit. I ended up laughing and asking the Lord to forgive me in my zeal without knowledge.

A Healing Word

At the retreat, sensing in my spirit that the Lord was directing me to a particular set of verses—John 16:20-24—I wondered whether I was really hearing from the Lord. Were there really twenty-four verses in chapter 16 of John's gospel? It was time to find out. With some reservations, I reluctantly picked up my Bible and opened it to John 16:20 and read these precious words:

> *Verily, verily, I say unto you, That ye shall weep and lament, but the world shall rejoice: and ye shall be sorrowful, but your sorrow shall be turned into joy. And ye now therefore have sorrow: but I will see you again, and your heart shall rejoice, and your joy no man taketh from you. And in that day ye shall ask me nothing. Verily, verily, I say unto you, Whatsoever ye shall ask the Father in my name, he will give it you. Hitherto have ye asked nothing in my name: ask, and ye shall receive that your joy may be full* (John 16:20,22-24).

Well this seemed to fit. It was my time of grief and sorrow. My sisters over in the cafeteria were all rejoicing while I was mourning. The good news was that Jesus said I could ask and the Father would not only hear me, but would also grant my request. I had a big request right then: I asked Him to restore my joy. Do you know, in a moment's time, I was delivered from sorrow and grief. The heavy spirit lifted from me and the life-giving joy of the Lord simply flooded my soul. The Bible tells us that the joy of the Lord is our strength. Believe me, I felt empowered and transformed. When I stood up, it was as if I had been washed totally clean. The anger was gone, the unforgiveness was gone, and the pain of the wounds from the Body of Christ had become bearable.

People of God, we must deal with our losses. Grief and sorrow come to us all in this life. Jesus said that in this world we will have tribulation, then He added, *"but be of good cheer; I have overcome the world"* (John 16:33b). He will be with us, helping us to go through the times of grief, and we must be open to His help. If we don't deal with the pain of our grief, it can turn into hidden bitterness. Yes, there will be a season of sorrow, but after some time has passed, we should be experiencing recovery.

Years of Pain

Let's look at a man in the Bible who also experienced loss. Jacob thought his son Joseph was dead when his other sons showed him the coat of many colors that had been torn and dipped in blood. *"And Jacob rent his clothes, and put on sackcloth upon his loins, and mourned for his son many days. And all his sons and all his daughters rose up to comfort him; but he refused to be comforted; and he said, For I will go down into the grave unto my son mourning. Thus his father wept for him"* (Genesis 37:34,35).

It is understandable that at the sudden death of his child, Jacob couldn't be comforted; however, as the years went by, it seems that his grief didn't diminish, but rather it intensified. Joseph was seventeen when he was sold into slavery. He was not delivered from prison and raised to the position Pharaoh's right-hand man until he was thirty. Then followed the seven years of abundance he had prophesied from Pharaoh's dream. It wasn't until the famine was well under way, so possibly a couple of years later, that Joseph's brothers traveled to Egypt looking for grain. Check it out. Over twenty years had passed since Joseph had reportedly been killed, and Jacob had spent those many years in deep grief.

For us to realize Jacob's feelings, we need to read the entire story, from Genesis 37 to Genesis 45. When the brothers returned from Egypt and said they needed to take Benjamin with them, Jacob wouldn't allow it. Benjamin was the only full brother of Joseph, and Jacob reminded his other sons many times over that he was still in sorrow over Joseph's death. If anything happened to Benjamin, Jacob's sorrow would bring his gray head to the grave. It seems that more than twenty years later, Jacob was in as much pain as he was at the beginning.

This story has a happy ending in that Jacob and Joseph were eventually reunited. Joseph told his brothers, *"But as for you, ye thought evil against me; but God meant it unto good, to bring to pass, as it is this day, to save much people alive. Now therefore fear ye not: I will nourish you, and your little ones. And he comforted them, and spake kindly unto them"* (Genesis 50:20,21). Joseph felt no bitterness because he trusted God. Jacob would have done well to exercise the same faith. It would have spared him years of sorrow and grieving. Remember, God is ready to heal us when we are ready to confess our own sins and receive His forgiveness.

How About You?

1. Are you experiencing pain over the loss of loved ones?

2. Are you blaming yourself or others for the grief you feel?

3. Bitterness had no part in Joseph's life although he had experienced betrayal from relatives, employers, and even fellow prisoners. Jesus also forgave His betrayers even while He was in agony from their betrayal. Can't you also forgive those who have betrayed you? When you forgive, you can be set free for a greater role in the Kingdom than "recorder of wrongs."

End Notes

1. The definitions for this section have been taken from both *The Bible Almanac*, edited by Packer, Tenney, and White, published by Thomas Nelson Publishers and *Strong's Exhaustive Concordance.*
2. *The Complete Word Study Old Testament*, AMG Publishers.

Chapter 9

Roots of Bitterness

Perhaps you saw the recent comedy take-off on the old Tarzan movies, *George of the Jungle*. The theme song went something like this: "George, George, George of the jungle strong as he could be... *Watch out for that tree!*" Forget the jungle and forget George, but that tree needs to be our focus—specifically, the roots of that tree. If we aren't on our guard, we don't necessarily smack into a tree, but those roots can definitely trip us up. The Word likens bitterness to a strong root that has really taken hold. The Bible instructs us, *"Follow peace with all men, and holiness, without which no man shall see the Lord: Looking diligently lest any man fail of the grace of God; lest any root of bitterness springing up trouble you, and thereby many be defiled"* (Hebrews 12:14,15).

When the Lord first dealt with me on the subject of bitterness being like a root, He used a memory from my childhood. We had a very large oak tree in our yard. It was probably close to 100 years old and was massive and beautiful. However, although it looked stately and proud, its roots caused great damage. They traveled underground as far as the sidewalk which led up to the front porch of our home. Obviously, they were hidden from sight, as most roots are, but gradually we began to notice a problem. It didn't happen all at once, or even overnight, but as the roots grew, the sidewalk began to crack. Portions of the cracked sidewalk began to tilt, and we were concerned about the hazard this presented. We were worried about the people trying to walk on our sidewalk and also about the law suits they might bring.

Dealing with the damage done by these roots proved difficult. They had taken years to develop and were too thick, too strong, and too far underground to be removed easily. We had to hire men with jackhammers to break up the broken sidewalk. Can you picture this in your mind?

Now consider the damage bitterness does in our lives. When I set out initially to look for roots of bitterness, I was reminded of this event from my childhood. I knew the Lord wanted me to uproot the bitterness before I became like the broken sidewalk, injuring myself and others.

We need to take a closer look at Hebrews 12:15 before we go any farther. The New International Version renders this verse *"See to it that no one misses the grace of God and that no bitter root grows up to cause trouble and defile many."* The Amplified Bible makes it even clearer: *"Exercise foresight and be on the watch to look (after one another) to see that no one falls back from and fails to secure God's grace (His unmerited favor and spiritual blessings) in order that no root of resentment (rancor, bitterness or hatred) shoot forth and cause trouble and bitter torment and that many become contaminated and defiled by it."*

Please notice that although this verse speaks of the damage bitterness can do, it also speaks of the grace of God. This is a key element for both preventing and overcoming bitterness. When bitter roots grow, we fall short of appropriating the grace needed to go through this bitter experience. Thank God for His amazing grace. As we prepare to lay the ax at the root of bitterness, we must keep focused on the fact that there's more than enough grace to see us through.

Searching Diligently

Another important element in this verse comes toward the end: the root of bitterness will trouble and hurt us, but it will also defile many others. How many of our friends and family members have been affected by our anger, resentment, and bitterness? We should be sympathetic to their suffering because we also have probably suffered due to the bitterness of someone else. Under the direction of the Holy Spirit, Paul wrote, *"Let all bitterness, and wrath, and anger, and clamour, and evil speaking, be put away from you, with all malice: And be ye kind one to another, tenderhearted, forgiving one another, even as God for Christ's sake hath forgiven you"* (Ephesians 4:31,32). This instruction is clear, yet I can't put away my bitterness or even offer forgiveness if I don't know what the roots are in my life. First, we must uncover the hidden roots of bitterness, and that may take some diligent searching.

How hard do we want to look for these roots? The answer to this is another question. How badly do we want to rid ourselves of this bitter root that is displeasing to God? We'll search diligently if it is of real importance in our lives. Consider this example:

A number of years ago, I went to the Islands—St. Thomas—to minister. My husband suggested that before I left, it would be a good idea if I only took one major credit card and left the others at home. I agreed with him and took all of my credit cards out of my wallet, put a rubber band around them, and hid them in a safe place.

Upon arriving back home, after the ministry trip, I wanted to retrieve my credit cards, but I couldn't remember where I had put them. They were safe all right—even from me! I looked and looked, and I prayed and prayed. My husband and I searched our house from top to bottom, but to no avail. We couldn't find them. I continued searching for weeks, but as I thought about how small they were compared to the size of our house, I gave up and ordered replacement cards.

It wasn't until a year later that we happened upon the hidden cards. I had put them in our nightstand among my husband's union papers. Once we found them, I could recall Boo sitting on our bed as we discussed my upcoming trip. I remember handing the cards to him and watching him put them away.

During the time that the cards were missing, even though I didn't physically look for them each and every day, I actually did a mental search for them almost daily. So it is with roots of bitterness. We may not search daily, but we should pray and allow the Holy Spirit to show us any hidden hindrances to our walk with God.

The Bitterness of Bondage

Let's unearth some roots. *"And they made their lives bitter with hard bondage"* (Exodus 1:14a). This verse is talking about the children of Israel during the time that they were in bondage to the Egyptians. The verse says that their lives were bitter *due to the bondage.* Roots of bitterness can develop as a result of anything that holds us in bondage.

One of the roots I struggled with was due to my addiction and bondage to cigarettes. Not long after my salvation, I became aware of the fact that my body was now the temple of God. I already knew that smoking was harmful to my body, but now that I realized my body belonged to God, my concern increased. Wanting to please Him in every way, I knew I needed to quit smoking; however, knowing you need to do something and actually *doing* it are two different things.

I struggled for months to quit, then decided I needed some outside help. So, every time there was an altar call, I was up front, asking for deliverance from the bondage of cigarettes. I remember being invited to a women's luncheon where, following the meal, the speaker was laying hands on those who wanted prayer and praying for them. I got in line thinking, *"Maybe this will be my day for deliverance."* As I approached the speaker, I lifted my hands toward heaven as an act of surrender to the Lord. The speaker pushed my hands back down and told me that God didn't want to see the nicotine stain on my hand. I began to cry, feeling very hurt by her response. Needless to say, I wasn't set free that day.

I tried to hide my smoking habit from my friends because I had become very ashamed of my addiction. I found myself as a grown woman, hiding in the bathroom in church and blowing the smoke into the toilet. (Memories of school days came flooding back.) Services at the church could last up to two hours, and I needed a cigarette break. I would then chew gum and return to the service. After the service, we would hug each other as a sign of Christian love. On another "memorable" day, a woman I hugged said to me "I'm glad you're not going to hell, because you smell like you've been there." Another lady told me that I would never be really filled with the Holy Spirit "because God won't fill a dirty vessel." With all of this free advice, I was ready to throw in the towel. Angry thoughts raced through my mind. "I'll smoke more than ever and go to heaven sooner than you"...and "If this is love, I'm sure glad you don't *dis*like me."

The root of bitterness grew, fed by my resentment. I was particularly frustrated when I saw new Christians who were delivered from smoking in a moment's time—without any struggle. Why was it so easy for them and so hard for me? I did everything that was suggested to me to help me quit smoking. By now I had carved a path in the rug at church leading to the altar. I was anointed with oil, I repented, I read books on deliverance and went after that spirit of nicotine; yet I remained in bondage. Well-meaning friends would share their testimonies of saying just one little prayer and never again wanting a cigarette. Well, whoopie for them! Here I was obsessed everyday, not noticing that I was as enslaved by the bitterness I hid as I was by the cigarettes—and the bitterness was infinitely more destructive than the nicotine.

I finally quit—not smoking, of course, but seeking God for this problem. Then, one day I was invited to a friend's house for lunch. During the course of our conversation, she asked me this question: "What is the one thing you would like the Lord to do for you? If you could have anything you asked, much like the offer He made to Solomon, what would you ask for?" My heart began to race. I knew what I wanted to ask for, but I feared another failure. The enemy had done a good job of convincing me that God really wasn't concerned with this problem and that I should just deal with it on my own. After all I had prayed and prayed about the smoking, and nothing had been resolved. (Am I the only one who has experienced this feeling of failure, or are you remembering a similar experience in your own life?)

I told my friend, Barbara, the tale of all my hurts and wounds, my failures and my disappointments. I told her of how I felt that I had let the Lord down and was such a poor witness for Him. Barbara ministered love, kindness, and forgiveness to me that day and asked if she could pray for me. I received her kindness gratefully, and thought "what could it hurt if she did pray for me." As soon as she prayed, however, I sensed a difference. I felt free. Being a doubting Thomas, I left her house expecting to crave a cigarette, but the craving never came.

Why had it taken so long for me to have my prayers answered? Why had He listened to Barbara's prayer? Her ministry to me gave me hope, but I think that her lovingkindness coincided with a more crucial element. As long as I liked to smoke, I couldn't get free. I think most of us who have bondages and addictions can relate to this. We either like what we are in bondage to or we feel we need it. Even though we may cry out for deliverance, we aren't really ready to let these things go. I had to get to the place where I was sick and tired of being sick and tired of my addiction.

Smoking is only my example. No matter what the bondage is—bitterness, anger, drugs, worry—if you will just continue to seek the Lord and pray, you can be set free. A helpful verse I used as a prayer is that for me *"sin by the commandment might become exceedingly sinful"* (Romans 7:13). I want you to know that God delivered me from a thirteen-year habit of smoking almost three packs a day. Not only that, but the real miracle for me was that after the first month of no cigarettes, I had lost four pounds. An addiction to overeating is also one that can develop in us a root of bitterness. After we fail on the many food fad plans and have been yo-yo dieters for years, it's hard to uncover the root of this compulsion—yet God would not have us enslaved to any addiction. We have been bought with a great price and should glorify God in our bodies. Enough for now on bondages. There are other roots to be unearthed.

The Bitterness Caused by Rebellion

"A foolish son is a grief to his father, and bitterness to her that bare him" (Proverbs 17:25). *"Thus saith the Lord; A voice was heard in Ramah, lamentation and bitter weeping: Rachel weeping for her children refused to be comforted for her children, because they were not"* (Jeremiah 31:15). I have two adult children, Mimi and Matthew, who are a tremendous blessing to me. My husband and I thank God for them now, but there was a short time when one of these blessings became a challenge as my daughter and I began to clash.

When Mimi entered her teen years, some rebellion began to surface. She felt we were too strict, and I know she resented us keeping her in a small Christian high school. My husband and I continued to maintain the discipline, but it was often painful and stressful to all of us. What I wasn't aware of was the fact that with each challenge, a little more was added to a hidden root of bitterness growing in me toward my own daughter.

I remember my mom saying to me, "You just wait till you have a daughter!" Only as a parent and an adult was I able to realize the extent of the hurt and heartache I had caused my mother. *"Whatever a man soweth, that shall he also reap"* (Galatians 6:7*b*). I am certainly living proof of this principle. One of the things I did in my young adolescent years that hurt my parents was that I was always attracted to kids that were trouble. As a parent, I could see this same pattern emerging in my daughter's life. It is not my intention to place blame on my daughter for all the discord we experienced. It takes two to tango, and tango we did. This incident will provide an excellent illustration.

Since my daughter's Christian school was very small, I knew most all her friends—at least, until a new girl who was Spanish came to the school. I had no problem with her being Spanish; after all, my husband is Hispanic, although he doesn't speak Spanish. Since I don't speak Spanish either, I couldn't call this girl's parents on the phone and introduce myself to them. They also lived forty minutes from us, making our communication even more difficult. Being friends in school was one thing, but when Mimi wanted to spend a weekend at this girl's house, I had to say no because I hadn't met the family and couldn't communicate with them. Mimi was really angry with me over this, and she stormed upstairs, slamming her bedroom door.

Some time later she came back downstairs, and there was a noticeable difference in her attitude. She told me of her anger and frustration in not being allowed to go to her friend's house for the weekend and said that she was going to jog around the block a few times to release her resentment. As she left the house, I began to think about what a good job of parenting Boo and I were doing. Our daughter was in touch with her feelings and understood how healthy it was to run and exercise in order to relieve stress.

Several minutes had passed and I was in the kitchen when my husband told me to quickly get in the car and drive around the block. He even told me the direction he wanted me to travel: "Gwen, go west, not east. Hurry up and drive around the block." This was an unusual request, but he was so urgent that I soon found myself grabbing my purse and car keys and running into the garage—still wearing my bedroom slippers, mind you.

As I turned the corner and drove down a quiet, deserted street, passing several houses, my headlights shone into the woods ahead. Out of the woods stepped my daughter, Mimi, carrying several duffel bags. I stopped the car, wondering what she was doing in the woods and what was all this stuff she was carrying. Mimi had a wide grin on her face—until she recognized the car. I was out of my car even faster than I had gotten in it.

Almost immediately a car pulled up behind me. It was her new Spanish friend.

Caught in the Act

It seems my daughter had decided to run away. She had called her friend from her bedroom phone and made plans for this friend to pick her up an hour later by the woods at the end of our block. Earlier, during the time spent in her room, she was packing her belongings and then lowering them out the window on a bedsheet. My kid's pretty gutsy because her bedroom window is directly over the window by our television, and my husband and I were watching TV the whole time this caper was going on. We never even noticed the descent of all the duffel bags.

The Bible tells us that God has the very hairs of our heads numbered. My daughter lost some that night as I helped my young blessing into the car. I then approached her new Spanish friend and shared the few Spanish words I knew. I told her she'd better Gracias Hay-soos! (Thank Jesus) that I couldn't call her folks and tell them about this little escapade. I strongly suggested she turn around and go home immediately.

This is only one incident that happened during those difficult years for my daughter and me. What I didn't realize is how much bitterness was developing in my heart with each new problem. Then came a day when during my Bible reading a verse from Lamentations really spoke to my heart: "*Your prophets have predicted for you falsehood and delusion and foolish things; and they have not exposed your iniquity and guilt to avert your captivity [by causing you to repent]*" (2:14a, Amplified Version). Somehow the Spirit of the Lord was warning me that this verse was to be applied to Mimi. The sun didn't even set that day before I received a call that there was some trouble at school and that Mimi was somehow involved. I don't want to go into specifics except to tell you that I knew I had to obey the Word of God. This was difficult because Mimi had managed to convince everyone of her innocence, including her darling dad.

I fasted and prayed because I didn't know how to do what I felt the

Lord wanted me to do. How do you expose someone else's sin, especially when everyone else is assuring you of her innocence? The Lord gave me wisdom and direction, and I was able to confront my daughter. I told Mimi that I knew she was guilty no matter what others believed—even her dad. I told her that Jesus had told me she was involved and that I was to expose this sin so she wouldn't be taken into captivity by a sin of a greater degree. Finally, I asked her if Jesus had lied to me. It was then that Mimi broke down and sobbed. After owning up to her part, she cried, "It's not fair! It's just not fair! Jesus tells you about everything I do!"

Parents, be encouraged that God not only loves you, but He is loving and caring for your children as well. Although Jeremiah 31:15 records that Rachel was weeping for her children and she refused to be comforted, the next verses contain a wonderful promise. "*Thus saith the Lord; Refrain thy voice from weeping, and thine eyes from tears: for thy work shall be rewarded, saith the Lord; and they shall come again from the land of the enemy. And there is hope in thy end, saith the Lord, that thy children shall come again to their own border*" (Jeremiah 31:16,17).

They shall come again from the land of the enemy. No matter what the enemy is doing or has done to your children, begin to claim this wonderful promise. It doesn't matter whether they've gotten into drugs, sex, abortion, rebellion, or any of the works of the enemy. Nothing is too difficult for God. Give them over to Him and have hope that the end will be better. Actually call them back from the land of the enemy. Boo and I did this for our children, and God honored His Word. My daughter is a beautiful woman and we now have a very loving and caring relationship. My son, Matthew, is in full-time ministry. Why? Because we refused to allow the enemy to have our offspring.

"*And did not God make [you and your wife] one [flesh]? Did not One make you and preserve your spirit alive? And why [did God make you two] one? Because He sought a godly offspring [from your union]*" (Malachi 2:15a, Amplified version). God is concerned about the marriage relationship because He is looking for godly offspring. The King James calls this godly seed. I went through the Scriptures and found many promises concerning the seed of the righteous being delivered. Psalm 127 tells us that *"children are an heritage from the Lord and the fruit of the womb is his reward"* (verse 3). Jeremiah tells us that the work we have done shall be rewarded through our children returning. We are also told, *"He is a rewarder of them that diligently seek him"* (Hebrews 11:6). Seek Him on behalf of your seed, and He will reward your faith and your labor.

Injustice, Relationships, and Bitterness

There is another root of bitterness that is currently doing tremendous damage to the church. We'll call it injustice by the brethren. Think back to the Biblical story of Esau and Jacob. Esau, being the firstborn, was in line for the double portion inherited by firstborn sons. His younger brother had stolen this blessing by deceiving their father. (See Genesis 27.) This is a heartbreaking story. Jacob's mother dresses him like his brother, Esau, and together Rebecca and Jacob lie, deceiving Isaac and swindling Esau out of his special blessing. Not only is Esau wounded by this, of course, but the entire family suffers. Bitterness affects everyone in the household.

Think of all the Biblical characters who experienced bitterness in their relationships: Esau and Jacob, Hagar and Sarah, Rachel and Leah, Joseph's brothers toward him. We already examined how the children of God quarreled with Moses and Aaron and how Aaron and Miriam resisted their brother. The Bible spends a great deal of time on the estrangement between Saul and David, and even David's own sons displayed great bitterness of heart. In fact, some of the most heinous crimes recorded in the Bible involve David's children.

For example, one of David's sons—Amnon—raped his half-sister, Tamar. Because of this crime, another of David's sons, Absalom, avenged Tamar by killing his brother, Amnon. After this murder, Absalom fled for his life. As time passed, David's heart ached for his son, and Absalom returned. However, little by little Absalom stole the hearts of the men and the servants of his father, and even tried to take over David's kingdom. (Read 2 Samuel 15 for the full story.) There are many other incidents of bitterness in the Bible, so why are we so surprised and stunned when bitterness towards one another appears among church member?

Lest we think the stories of bitterness are confined to the Old Testament, remember how the other ten disciples were bitter towards James and John? The brothers had asked their mother to approach Jesus concerning giving them preferential seats. *"Grant that these my two sons may sit, the one on thy right hand, and the other on the left, in thy kingdom"* (Matthew 20:21*b*). The man at the pool of Bethesda was bitter that when the angel stirred the water for healing, someone always got to the pool before he did. (See John 5:2-7.) Even Mary and Martha had some bitterness between them. *"Martha was cumbered about with much serving, and came to him, and said, Lord, dost thou not care that my sister hath left me to serve alone? Bid her therefore that she help me"* (Luke 10:40). The book of Ephesians was written to the church, and it tells us *"let all bitterness, and wrath, and anger, and clamour, and evil speaking, be put away from you, with all malice"* (4:31). Why would Paul have given the church members this instruction if they didn't need it? (Often we want to be like the Early Church, but there are some practices we don't want to imitate.)

I have already shared some hurts through relationship problems or thoughtless words on the part of believers. Another incident may alert you to the subtlety of the enemy. I am ashamed to say that it took me over four years to recover from the bitterness caused by this particular wound.

Who's the Real Leader?

My husband and I belonged to a fellowship that was growing and moving beautifully in God; however, with the growth came growing pains. Some changes caused us much concern, and several times we spoke to leadership, being careful not to cause division in the body. At the time, I was teaching in a Bible school that was sponsored and supported by this church, but I didn't realize how many members looked at me as a leader due to my position in the school.

One Sunday morning, there were several words of prophecy during the worship time. One after another, these prophecies were shared until finally one brother said that Satan was dead. That shocked me, and my husband and I sat down, fully expecting the pastor or elder to correct this brother who was seriously in error. Nothing was done and the service continued, yet the Bible clearly tells us to judge prophecy. Even with a very small knowledge of the Bible, anyone but an infant would know that Satan isn't dead. There was definitely a problem here.

We were not aware that when we sat down, many in the congregation behind us were watching us—and they also sat down. It was only a few days after this service that we got a phone call that the Pastor wanted to see us. When we entered the Pastor's office, not only was he there but also his wife and two elders. The Pastor told us to leave the church. My husband tried to reason with him, telling him that God had put us into this local church and had not released us to leave. The Pastor told us he didn't care. We were to leave HIS church. I was so upset I was shaking and trying with all my heart not to cry. When my husband saw that his efforts were futile, we stood to leave. One elder announced, "Let's pray." I thought he couldn't be serious. After this type of meeting you want to pray? Pray about what? The four of them had made this decision, and it seemed we were powerless to change their minds. I not only couldn't pray with them, but I couldn't even stay in the room. I simply fled, and my husband followed me outside. I broke down and sobbed. What had we done? We didn't even know what the problem was or what charges they had against us. Put out of a church! I couldn't believe this.

When we reached home, I asked my husband to call the deacons to see if there had been some meeting of the leaders that brought the pastor and elders to their decision. He spoke to about nine of the deacons, and no one knew anything of what had just transpired. I didn't know what to do, where to go, who to call; and because this church was independent, there was no one to appeal to for what we felt was rank injustice.

I was devastated. My husband tried to comfort me, telling me the

Lord would fight this battle, and He would vindicate us. "When and how?" was what I wanted to know. It wasn't until after we were asked to leave that other folks began to call us and tell us that the very same thing had happened to them. It seems that if the Pastor couldn't control you, he removed you.

I was just sick about the whole situation. I wanted to be able to truly forgive because I knew that's what Jesus wanted for me, but I couldn't even mouth the words. I wrote letters to my friends in the fellowship to explain that the only reason I wouldn't be attending the church was that Pastor had asked us to leave. I wanted my friends to do something on my behalf. I wanted a trial—mainly because I was so frustrated at being sentenced without even knowing the charges against me. To add insult to my injury, people we had gone to church with for years, who had sat next to us, had prayed with us, had sat under my teachings, had eaten meals with us, had sung "Bind Us Together, Lord" with us, didn't do anything. A few called, but that was about it.

Obviously I made many mistakes in the way I handled this rejection. As I look back, the letters were written as a cry for help. I should have known that my help is in the Lord and cried more to Him and less to His people. My friends felt powerless to do anything, so—like most of us—they did nothing.

The Lord Is My Lifeline...

In the midst of my many mistakes, there was one thing I did right. I went to another church. We never missed a Sunday of worshiping together with God's people. I am so glad that I didn't have bitterness toward the Lord. Had we sulked and stayed at home, we would have allowed the devil to put us in a place of isolation. I needed healing and many times this healing comes from the very ones who have wounded us—but I was so afraid to trust anyone.

Our new Pastor was an understanding man, and God used his gentle spirit as a balm of Gilead for me. Although my spirit was trying to heal, my flesh was on the warpath. I was angry, resentful, bitter. I couldn't even pray for my ex-Pastor, though the Bible says we are to pray for those who have hurt us. "*But I say unto you, Love your enemies, bless them that curse you, do good to them that hate you, and pray for them which despitefully use you, and persecute you; That ye may be the children of your Father which is in heaven: for he maketh his sun to rise on the evil and on the good, and sendeth rain on the just and on the unjust*" (Matthew 5:44,45). Sadly, the only prayer I could pray for my ex-Pastor at this time was "God, get him." My daily Bible reading tended to be the Psalms, particularly those verses David wrote calling for vengeance on his enemies.

I wish I could say that it took only a short time for the Holy Spirit to enable me to let go of this hurt, but that was not the case. Even though I knew better, it was so hard to forgive and release this issue. Paul says in Romans 7, "*The good that I would I do not: but the evil which I would not, that I do*" (verse 19). "*But I see another law in my members, warring against the law of my mind, and bringing me into captivity to the law of sin which is in my members. O wretched man that I am! Who shall deliver me from the body of this death?*" (verses 23,24).

Like Paul, I also asked who would deliver me; and then the answer came: Jesus. Jesus is the answer to our letting go, our forgiving, and our wounds being healed, and our releasing the hurts. After what seemed like a lifetime, I was able to pray 2 Timothy 4:16 with sincerity of heart: "*At my first answer no man stood with me, but all men forsook me: I pray God that it may not be laid to their charge.*"

I'd like you to consider something I find very interesting. The longer we are Christians, the less likely it is that we will hold grudges against those who are not believers. Why is this? We tend to expect less and less of those who have not yet been saved. We do expect more and more, however, of those who profess to follow Christ. It stands to reason, then, that it is usually the family of God, our brothers and sister in Christ, who have given us pain. But we can't use that as an excuse to harbor bitterness. Let me ask you something. Are you perfect yet? Do you *never* say or do things that offend others? Never have a bad day? When Jesus asked the one who was without sin to cast the first stone, He could have been talking to each of us.

Friend, the misery of unforgiveness is like plant food to those roots of bitterness. Why struggle any longer? If we want the abundant life Jesus promised us and the total joy of living in God's presence, if we want to absolutely delight the heart of God, we must forgive those who have hurt us.

How About You?

1. Think about the roots that may exist in your life. What will you do with roots of bitterness? Will you continue to unearth these roots, under the guidance of the Holy Spirit, or will you cover them up?

2. Think back to your childhood. Were you ever a source of bitterness to your parents? Has there been any bitter rivalry among your family members? Invite the Lord to bring healing and show you any steps you need to take or prayers you need to pray in order to be reconciled with your family. You might want to pray first for the grace to obey what He shows you to do.

3. Do you know someone who has been injured or hurt by others in the Church? Perhaps that someone is you. In either case, God will supply the strength and grace needed for forgiveness to flow. This is usually a process. Be patient and make yourself available for His working through you. Continue to pray daily until you find a release.

4. Is there ever a time we are justified in holding on to bitterness? Do you think Jesus was tempted to be bitter? Did He hold on to bitterness?

Chapter 10

The Ax at the Root

If you can read only one chapter in my book, this should be the chapter you read. The concepts presented here are the most important of all. We have stressed the need for forgiveness, but now I'd like us to take a closer look at this issue. What *is* forgiveness, and what is its connection with bitterness? How do I know if I have really forgiven, or if I have only said I forgive? Do my heart and my head have to agree for true forgiveness to take place? What if the other person won't admit his or her fault? Do I still have to forgive? Is it okay to forgive over and over again for the same affliction? Must I also forget?

We're not only going to look at forgiveness, but we will look at steps to restoration once we have gone through the entire forgiveness process. If the other person refuses to be reconciled, there are steps to bring closure to the offense and also ways to be certain we rid ourselves of any residue of unforgiveness. I'd like to begin, however, with what happens to us when we don't forgive.

The story of Jacob and Esau will illustrate this issue for us. You remember that Jacob deceived his brother and stole his blessing; however, Esau isn't without fault because he sold his birthright to Jacob. (I truly believe that there are few times when only one person is to blame.) Do you know what a birthright is and how you can sell it? This is a foreign concept to most of us, but the Bible implies it was a very serious matter.

I'll quickly summarize Genesis 25:27-34 where this particular issue arises. Jacob is cooking and Esau comes in hungry from his work in the field. When Esau smells what's cooking, he says to Jacob, "Feed me for I am faint."

Jacob replies, "I'll feed you if you sell me this day thy birthright." The Bible goes on to say that Esau despised his birthright and for one meal he sold what should have been precious and priceless to him. Yes, Jacob was wrong in not giving his brother a free meal, but Esau was in sin because he didn't hold his birthright in high esteem.

We have quoted Hebrews 12:15, the root-of-bitterness verse, in several chapters, but read the verse again and also the verses that follow it:

Looking diligently lest any man fail of the grace of God; lest any root of bitterness springing up trouble you, and thereby many be defiled: Lest there be any fornicator or profane person, as Esau, who for one morsel of meal sold his birthright. For ye know how that afterward, when he would have inherited the blessing, he was rejected: for he found no place of repentance, though he sought it carefully with tears (verses 15-17).

This strikes a chord. How many of us are sorry after the fact? We may be tearful, but sometimes it seems too late.

God did a work in both brothers' hearts before complete forgiveness flowed from one to the other. Years went by and God told Jacob he must return home to Esau. The story of their reunion is found in Genesis, chapter 32. Before we proceed with a detailed analysis, we must remember one really important fact: Years went by before they were reconciled. While I'm not saying that every reconciliation will take years, we are foolish to assume that forgiveness will occur instantly in every case. Sometimes we want to immediately forgive, forget, and move on as though nothing had ever happened. On the rare occasion, this may work, but wisdom dictates we seek God in these matters and submit ourselves to His divine timing. Did you know that King David was offended by his son Absalom, and after Absalom fled from his father's presence, it took two years for David's heart to once again yearn for his son? (Please don't use this story to go into denial for two years because you're just asking to enter the Land of Torment. Trust me. You don't even want to visit that village!)

Steps toward Restoration

Going back to the reunion of Esau and Jacob as related in Genesis 32, the first thing I want to look at is this: *"And Jacob sent messengers before him to Esau his brother unto the land of Seir, the country of Edom. And he commanded them, saying, Thus shall ye speak unto my lord Esau; Thy servant Jacob saith thus…"* (verse 3, 4a). Jacob instructs these messengers to tell his brother of all that he has accomplished since their parting, all the years he worked for Laban, all the wealth he has acquired. The important thing is not his past but that he calls Esau his lord, himself Esau's servant, and Jacob asked for grace. *"I have sent to tell my lord, that I may find grace in thy sight"* (verse 5b).

Step one involves humility. Jacob saw himself under Esau, as his servant. Before there can be restoration, one of the two parties has to be willing to humble himself and obey God.

The second step involves asking for grace. I see this as being very closely tied to the third step of dealing with our fears. *"And the messengers returned to Jacob, saying, We came to thy brother Esau, and also he cometh to meet thee, and four hundred men with him. Then Jacob was greatly afraid and distressed"* (verses 6 and 7a). The word *afraid* in this passage pertains to the fear of what might go wrong. How many times have you and I allowed the fear of what *might* happen to paralyze us—and so we haven't even approached the other person. Even when we humble ourselves and ask for grace, we must overcome the fear of how the other person will receive us. If we don't, we'll likely be so tense that the next words out of their mouths will hurt or offend us.

We know we need to humble ourselves, ask for grace, and overcome fear. How do we do this? Step four—we pray, as Jacob did. *"And Jacob said, O God of my father Abraham, and God of my father Isaac, the Lord which saidst unto me, Return unto thy country, and to they kindred, and I will deal well with thee: I am not worthy of the least of all the mercies, and of all the truth, which thou hast shewed unto thy servant"* (verses 9,10a). Jacob humbled himself before God, recognizing that he was not worthy of all the mercy God had shown him.

Step five—always remember that God is a God of grace and mercy, and remind Him of His mercy. Our attitudes need to be right before God. If we take His blessings and mercies for granted, we will probably have a less than humble spirit before Him.

God is so worthy of our worship. Realizing this, we know we don't need to be fearful or even anxious. In fact, worry is a sin. The Bible commands us *"Do not fret or have any anxiety about anything, but in every circumstance and in everything, by prayer and petition (definite requests), with thanksgiving, continue to make your wants known to God"* (Philippians 4:6, Amplified version).

Step six—Jacob asked for deliverance. *"Deliver me, I pray thee, from the hand of my brother..."* (verse 11). Jacob reminded God of his obedience to what the Lord had commanded and that God had promised He would deal well with him. Never forget that if you trust God and do as He instructs you, He will see to it that it will go well for you.

After praying, Jacob *"lodged there that same night; and took of that which came to his hand a present for Esau his brother"* (verse 13). Step seven—send a gift or present. Could this be Scriptural? Jacob's reason is found in verse 20: "*…For he said, I will appease him with the present that goeth before me, and afterward I will see his face; peradventure he will accept of me.*" Knowing his brother was likely to be angry, Jacob figured he would prepare his brother's heart by sending a gift. Look at what these other verses say. "*A man's gift maketh room for him, and bringeth him before great men*" (Proverbs 18:16). "*A gift in secret pacifieth anger: and a reward in the bosom strong wrath*" (Proverbs 21:14).

Winning a Sister

I'd like to share a time when I used this principle from God's Word to win an offended sister. I was attending an Assembly of God church, and one of the women who had been there for years and years was offended when I, a newcomer, was asked to teach the Ladies' Bible Study during the Pastor's absence. I feel sure there were other things that I did unintentionally that annoyed her. When the Lord showed me her feelings toward me, I could have just shrugged it off as her problem. But I knew that God didn't want her to harbor ill feelings toward me. Jesus deals with this specifically in the Sermon on the Mount. "*If when you are offering your gift at the altar you there remember that your brother has any [grievance] against you, Leave your gift at the altar and go. First make peace with your brother, and then come back and present your gift*" (Matthew 5:23,24, Amplified version).

The problem was that I just didn't know how to approach her. As I prayed and waited on the Lord for direction, He told me to give her a gift. I'll be honest. She wasn't one of my favorite people either, so what could I give her? I finally decided on some lovely stationery that had Scripture verses on each page. I wrapped the box, attached a thinking-of-you card, and put it on her chair the next Sunday morning. You would have thought by her reaction that I had spent hundreds of dollars on her. From that day on, we had a healing in our relationship and became friends. A gift works wonders.

Back to our brothers. In Genesis 33, Jacob sees his brother, Esau, approaching with four hundred men. Jacob bows to Esau seven times,

"And Esau ran to meet him, and embraced him, and fell on his neck, and kissed him: and they wept" (verse 4). Esau tells Jacob to keep his gift, that Esau has enough. *"And Jacob said, Nay, I pray thee, if now I have found grace in thy sight, then receive my present at my hand: for therefore I have seen thy face, as though I had seen the face of God, and thou wast pleased with me"* (verse 10). Jacob linked his brother forgiving him and being pleased with him to God, and I feel sure that God was pleased with both of them.

This story has a happy ending, but regardless of the outcome of our attempts to reconcile, the important part is that we obey God's every instruction. Even if restoration doesn't take place, there are things we need to do to remove unforgiveness and bitterness. What if the person we have been estranged from dies? What then?

Forgive, forgive, forgive! *"Let all bitterness, and wrath, and anger, and clamour, and evil speaking, be put away from you, with all malice: And be ye kind one to another, tenderhearted, forgiving one another, even as God for Christ's sake hath forgiven you"* (Ephesians 4:31,32). Notice the words *even as*. "Even as God for Christ's sake has forgiven you." The first reason we need to forgive is so that our own sins will be forgiven. As we forgive our brother, God forgives us. Don't we see this in the Lord's Prayer? *"And forgive us our debts as we forgive our debtors"* (Matthew 6:12) Right after the Lord's Prayer, Jesus explains, *"For if ye forgive men their trespasses, your heavenly Father will also forgive you: But if ye forgive not men their trespasses, neither will your Father forgive your trespasses"* (Matthew 6:14,15). What we need to remember during those times when it's hard to forgive is that if we don't forgive, we aren't forgiven either. I don't know about you, but I need to know that my sins and debts are forgiven.

Confession Time

Growing up as a Roman Catholic, I was taught from a very young age that I shouldn't go into a Protestant church. I had only attended Catholic churches—and Catholic schools—until one summer afternoon when I was a young girl. My family had just come home from Mass, and I went out to play. There was a Baptist church around the corner from my house, and since it was the middle of the summer, they had the doors open while they were having service. I paused in my play, hearing the most beautiful music in the world coming from inside that church.

You must remember that this was back in the '50s, long before the Mass was in English or the Catholic Church had experienced the renewal movement of the '70s. We didn't normally have any music during our Sunday service, so I was curious about what I was hearing. I drew closer and closer to the building, when all of a sudden, a big man in a black suit appeared at the back door and invited me in. I told him I was a Catholic, and he responded that the Baptists love the same Jesus that the Catholics do. He invited me to come in and sing.

I entered this foreign land, and a hymnal was handed to me. All the people were singing "What a Friend We Have in Jesus," and my heart was so touched that tears rolled down my fat little cheeks. However, when I left the building, I had a terrible weight on my shoulders because I realized what I had done. I had committed a sin by entering a Protestant church. I ran home crying and told my mother my sin. She was very upset and began to beat her chest, saying over and over, "Jesus, Mary, and Joseph have mercy!" The next thing I knew, my two aunts—the ones who are nuns—joined Mom. I was crying about how sorry I was, and everyone was praying for me. My mother finally looked me in the eye and told me that she hoped Jesus would allow me to live until next Saturday night so I could go to confession.

Because of the tradition of the Catholic church at that time, I thought I had removed all of God's grace on my soul by this sin; and should I die before I could confess this sin to a priest, I would go to hell. I lived all week with a sick sense that my sin wasn't forgiven. I counted the days until Saturday, and you can be sure I lived the straight and narrow *that* week. Before this, I must confess that I used to steal a little change from my dad's dresser every now and then—more now than then. But during my week of waiting for confession, every penny was accounted for. Finally Saturday came and I was able to go to confession, do my penance, and feel forgiven.

I don't share this to offend Catholics—and I hope I haven't offended any—but to tell you that I still remember that time when I thought God hadn't forgiven me. The Word of God tells us if we don't forgive, we aren't forgiven. I don't know about you, but I will never again wait a week, living in unforgiveness. I know now that I can confess my sins directly to God at any time and at any place, and He is faithful and just to forgive and to cleanse me of all my sins. How good it feels to know I am clean in His sight as long as I walk in accordance with His Word. Since I need forgiveness on a daily basis, I must be quick to forgive my brother, so that my Father can forgive me.

An Unholy Advantage

The second reason to forgive is one that the Body of Christ seems to overlook. We are so busy reading books on spiritual warfare and attending conferences where we storm the gates of hell. But, while we are coming against the enemy, we have left the back door open to him. There's a passage that is often overlooked in 2 Corinthians chapter 2. "*To whom ye forgive any thing, I forgive also: for if I forgave any thing, to whom I forgave it, for your sakes, forgave I it in the person of Christ;* <u>*Lest Satan should get an advantage of us*</u>*: for we are not ignorant of his devices*" (verses 10,11, emphasis added).

Satan gets the advantage over us if we don't forgive, and I think many of us are ignorant of his device of unforgiveness. I can't afford him having any advantage over me, can you? This is particularly crucial in these last days when God's Word says that many will be deceived. So many times when we are struggling to forgive, we keep looking at the other person. We need to look at ourselves and these first two vital points: Forgive so you can be forgiven and forgive so that Satan doesn't get the advantage over you. Remember, he has had thousands of years to perfect his devices, and through ignorance we can enter into deception. Do you really want to give the devil the upper hand? If you choose not to forgive, you have given him the advantage of a terrible hold over you.

Forgive from Your Heart

The third reason to forgive is found in Matthew 18. There are a couple of verses in this chapter that very few of us have committed to memory. *"And his lord was wroth, and delivered him to the tormentors, till he should pay all that was due unto him. So likewise shall my heavenly Father do also unto you, if ye from your hearts forgive not every one his brother their trespasses"* (verses 34,35). This verse doesn't say the *devil* turned you over to be tormented; it says that the Heavenly Father will do this if we don't forgive. I don't know about you, but I don't like torment—and this verse says we will be given over to the tormentors *plural*. The Amplified Bible says that he was turned over to the torturers (the jailers). Whenever we don't forgive, we are tortured and tormented. Isn't this ironic? Here we are thinking we are punishing the person we're mad at by withholding our forgiveness. In actuality, we are punishing ourselves.

I once had a very difficult time forgiving a woman who repeatedly hurt me. I hardened my heart and didn't forgive. For almost two full years, I lived in the land of torment and was tortured with bitterness, anger, and resentment. Everywhere I turned, there she was. When I spoke at a dinner for Christians, who do you think they asked to sing before I ministered. You guessed it. I began to think of her as my thorn in the flesh because although I tried over and over to release her, I remained in prison. While she was free, there I was feeling bound in chains.

The truths presented in Matthew 18 about binding and loosing actually deal with forgiveness and unforgiveness. Jesus began to tell us there how to handle offenses that will happen to us in the Body of Christ. Beginning in verse 15, we read, *"Moreover if thy brother shall trespass against thee, go and tell him his fault between thee and him alone: if he shall hear thee, thou hast gained thy brother."*

Two important things are often overlooked in this instruction from verse 15. First, you aren't supposed to tell others of the offense. Second, your purpose in this is to win back your brother and restore your relationship. Sad to say, one of the most common mistakes we make is telling others, even if we share it by calling it a prayer request. When we tell our sad, offended story to others, we tend to relive the hurt. This only causes it to grow bigger and deeper. The second common mistake is that we focus on the part about telling him his fault, and not on the part about winning him back. Even the Bible says the first person to speak will appear correct and that when we repeat a matter, we separate friends. If Sally hurts me and I tell Jeannie before I go to Sally, the next time Jeannie sees Sally, she will remember the things I shared with her. If Jeannie and I are close, she will be sorely tempted to pick up the offense and defend me—and poor Sally won't have a clue why she feels tension whenever she's around Jeannie.

When you have sought the other person one on one, and have found that the situation can't be resolved between the two of you, then and only then would someone else be included in this restoration. This other person is to serve as a witness, and I emphasize the word *witness*. This third person shouldn't be informed before you go into all the particular juicy details, or you have just set them up. This person is rather to witness the two of you who ought to be trying to resolve the problem between you. If after the two of you and a witness still can't bring closure to this trespass, then you tell the church.

Binding and Loosing

The next text we need to apply is from verse 18 of this passage in Matthew. *"Verily I say unto you, Whatsoever ye shall bind on earth shall be bound in heaven: and whatsoever ye shall loose on earth shall be loosed in heaven."* This is the doctrine of binding and loosing. You see, the binding is unforgiveness, and the loosing is forgiveness. If I don't forgive you here on earth, heaven is bound. You can still be forgiven by God, but heaven is bound. If I won't forgive you out of my own free will, even God can't make me; therefore, what I have bound on earth is bound in heaven. The same is true of forgiveness. If I forgive, we are both loosed—here on earth as well as in heaven. One thing I have learned from living in the land of torment is that I was bound to the person I hadn't forgiven, always thinking about her and the offense, wondering would she be in church, or in

Bible study. Should I say hello, or act like I didn't see her?

Now we come to one of the most misinterpreted verses in the New Testament. So many of us—including yours truly—have taken this text out of its setting and applied it to situations it has absolutely nothing to do with. *"For where two or three are gathered together in my name, there am I in the midst of them"* (Matthew 18:20). Whenever the attendance at a prayer breakfast was small, or it rained on a Sunday morning, we have quoted this verse. We assured each other, "Jesus is here because two or three of us have gathered in His name." Well, I'm here to tell you that Jesus is there if only one person comes, because if that person is saved, Jesus lives in them. Everywhere I go, I go with the One who indwells me. The essence of this scripture deals with the two who are trying, along with the witness, to resolve their problem so it doesn't have to go before the whole church. Jesus is in the midst so they can forgive each other and be reconciled. Hallelujah!

We are ready to look at the story of the people God will send into the land of torment, those who will be bound in prison. The parable is found in Matthew 18:22-35. I am going to tell it in my own words, but I would first like to point out to you verse 27: *"Then the lord of that servant was moved with compassion, and loosed him, and forgave him the debt."* Just keep that phrase in mind.

One day a king wanted to see how his servants were doing, and he wanted his outstanding debts collected. The first servant brought to him owed the king millions of dollars, and when payday came, he couldn't pay his debt to the king. He fell down before the king and assured him that he would pay him back in full if the king would only have patience with him. The king was moved with compassion and released, or loosed him, of the entire debt.

The servant who was forgiven of this huge debt went out and he came across a fellow servant who owed him a few dollars. He grabbed the guy by the throat and began to choke him, demanding his money right then and there. The poor fellow asked for mercy and patience, saying he would repay all. (This is even more significant than when the first servant asked the king for patience. It is one thing for us to fall before a king and ask for mercy, but it is quite another to fall before a fellow servant.) The man who was loosened from his gigantic debt would not loose his fellow servant from his miniscule debt. Instead, he put the poor guy in prison, intending to sell whatever the man might own to pay his debt.

The other servants witnessed this injustice, and they did something I pray that we will learn to do. Grieved and saddened over the strife between the two servants, they went to the king and told him what had happened.

The meaning of this parable is that God is our king, and none of us could ever repay Him. In His love and mercy, He has forgiven us so much. Shouldn't we also then forgive each other? If we don't, we may end up in the same position as the unforgiving servant who was thrown into prison to be tormented.

Was the unforgiving man in this parable called a wicked servant because he had a debt to pay in the first place? No. Was he wicked because he humbled himself and asked for patience? No. He was called wicked because he refused to loose his brother. After he had been set free, he put his fellow servant into prison; but who ended up doing the time? He did. We need to remember this.

There are many words we use to express forgiveness: to pardon, to free, to cancel a debt. What we may fail to realize from these synonyms is that the word *forgive* also means **to give up the wish to get even**. I have the option of choosing to forgive. When I take that option, what I am saying to God is that I give up the wish to get even with them for what they did to me. May God help each of us to be aware that with the measure we use it will be measured back to us again.

"But love ye your enemies, and do good, and lend, hoping for nothing

again; and your reward shall be great, and ye shall be the children of the Highest: for he is kind unto the unthankful and to the evil. Be ye therefore merciful, as your Father also is merciful" (Luke 6:35,36). If we can't even forgive our brethren, how will we be able to forgive our enemies? Lord, please work in each of our hearts; and thank You for Your great mercy to us.

There are other decisions we can make. On many occasions when we have been hurt, we look at the other person or we look at the offense. Let's turn that around and look at ourselves. "Do I really want God to turn me over to the tormenters? Do I want Him to no longer forgive my sins? Do I want Satan to have an advantage over me?" The answers to each of these questions is No. Keep these things in your mind the next time you are tempted to take offense. Oh yes! There will be future offenses. Jesus said, *"It is impossible but that offences will come..."* (Luke 17:1).

How Do We Forgive?

Now that we are convinced that we must forgive, let's look at *how* we need to forgive. Jesus also said, *" Woe unto him through whom [the offenses] come! It were better for him that a millstone were hanged about his neck, and he cast into the sea, than that he should offend one of these little ones. Take heed to yourselves"* (Luke 17:1b-3a). We certainly don't want to be the ones through whom the offense comes. Jesus tells his disciples to watch out for themselves, and believe me, that is still good advice for us today. *"If thy brother trespass against thee, rebuke him; and if he repent, forgive him. And if he trespass against thee seven times in a day, and seven times in a day turn again to thee, saying, I repent; thou shalt forgive him"* (Luke 17: 3b,4). I am pretty sure that this is where Peter got the idea to ask Jesus the following question: *"How oft shall my brother sin against me, and I forgive him? till seven times?"* (Matthew 18:21)

Of course, we know the answer that Jesus gave him. "No, Peter, not seven times but seven times seventy." Does that mean that when you cross off the 490th offense and you reach offense #491 I should put a millstone around your neck and drop you into the sea? Only you can answer that question! After Jesus tells His disciples about offenses and rebuking and repenting, they make a profound utterance: *"Lord, increase our faith"* (Luke 17:5).

The best way to forgive anyone at any time is to do it by faith. Too many of us try to forgive by feelings, and that's where we get into trouble. Faith is not a feeling. I choose to forgive you, I give up the wish to get even with you, and I do so because of my faith in God and His Word. When faith is released, the feeling will eventually come; but don't wait to forgive until you *feel* forgiveness. Don't keep praying, "Lord, help me to forgive." Instead, pray in this way: "Lord, increase my faith to forgive."

The second aid in forgiving is found in the gospel of St. John 20:22,23. Jesus had been resurrected from the dead, however, his disciples still feared the Jews. The disciples had gathered together behind locked doors. All of a sudden, Jesus was there with them and said, *"Peace be to you."* After He showed them His hands and His side, they believed it was really Jesus. What Jesus did next is of the utmost importance to each of us. He breathed on them, and said, *"Receive the Holy Ghost."* We have made so many doctrines on the breath of the Holy Spirit, and yet few have ever understood why the Holy Spirit was breathed on them. It wasn't so they could start a Pentecostal church. The reason the Holy Spirit was breathed into them is so that they could have supernatural power to forgive.

"And having said this, He breathed on them and said to them, Receive (admit) the Holy Spirit! [Now having received the Holy Spirit, and being led and directed by Him] if you forgive the sins of anyone, they are forgiven; if you retain the sins of anyone, they are retained" (John 20:22,23, Amplified Version). The NIV expresses the last part *"if you do not forgive them, they are not forgiven."* Can you see the logical sequence here? We don't want there to be any language barrier to understanding. Some translations use the words *remit* and *retain*. To remit simply means to dismiss, forsake and forgive. To retain means to hold on to. We have the power, given to us by the Holy Spirit, to dismiss and forgive sins or to hold on to

them. Jesus set the best example, saying, *"Father, forgive them, for they know not what they do…"* (Luke 23:34). If He did not retain the grievance, how then can we? But, you might argue, He said we didn't know what we were doing. It's harder to forgive someone who knows full well they are doing wrong and do it anyway. That's where bitterness comes in.

Some of you have been reading this entire book hoping I'll address this issue and you'll be off the hook. I'm going to share with you what the Word says because Jesus has an answer for this very important question, too. We need to look for one minute at the life of Stephen. He was a deacon in the early church, and the Bible says he was *"…a man full of faith and of the Holy Ghost…And Stephen, full of faith and power, did great wonders and miracles among the people"* (Acts 6:5,8). Although Stephen was a good and righteous man, full of the Holy Spirit, the Jewish leaders determined he was a threat to them and they stoned him to death. As he was dying, he forgave the people who had killed him. *"And he kneeled down, and cried with a loud voice, Lord, lay not this sin to their charge…"* (Acts 7:60).

Can you imagine doing this, releasing love and forgiveness while the stones are breaking your very bones? The reason he was able to forgive his murderers is that he was full of the Holy Spirit, and in his pain he saw Jesus. The Bible says that as his murderers rushed at him, gnashing their teeth with fury, Stephen, *"being full of the Holy Ghost, looked up stedfastly into heaven, and saw the glory of God, and Jesus standing on the right hand of God"* (Acts 7:55). Whenever the New Testament speaks of Jesus at the right hand of God, it says He is *seated* there. When Stephen is about to die, Jesus stood up for him so he could forgive. <u>Although our flesh would find it very difficult to forgive, Jesus and the Holy Spirit will enable us to do what we could not do on our own.</u>

Jesus Forgives in Us, through Us, and for Us

A third assistance we have in forgiving is found in 2 Corinthians 2:10*b*: *"to whom I forgave it, for your sakes forgave I it in the person of Christ."* The person of Christ is involved in our forgiveness because Jesus can forgive in us, through us, and for us. With His Spirit and love, we can forgive the unforgivable. When it seems humanly impossible to forgive, He will enable us to do what would otherwise be impossible. Can a father forgive a man who abused his daughter? Can a mother hold no unforgiveness against the murderer of her child? These are extreme examples, but no matter what has been done to or against us, we can go to Jesus and ask Him to help us to forgive. He will rise for the occasion so that we can be like Him.

It's worth repeating that there are times that our forgiveness will be there instantly, by the grace of God and our determination to please Him. There are also times when the forgiveness may involve many steps and be a lengthy process. As long as we are committed to doing what Jesus would have us do, and rely on the helps He has provided, we will have victory in this area of forgiveness.

The choice is ours, will we be like Jesus, or will we hold onto bitterness and be like the enemy? We are to prepare the way of the Lord much as John the Baptist did. "*Bring forth therefore fruits meet for repentance…And now also the axe is laid unto the root of the trees: therefore every tree which bringeth not forth good fruit is hewn down, and cast into the fire*" (Matthew 3:8,10). The only way for us to have our roots of bitterness removed is for us to produce fruits of repentance—then the ax is laid at the root, then we can be delivered from being a tool in the hand of the enemy.

We can't change our past or the wounds we have suffered, but we have plenty of say in our future. I no longer shift the blame to other people when I am offended, hurt, or wounded. I look inward and upward: inward so that I repent of the unforgiveness, bitterness, and anger that made up my initial response, and upward to Jesus, the finisher of my faith. Furthermore, believers have been given the fruit of the Spirit: "*But the fruit of the Spirit is love, joy, peace, longsuffering, gentleness, goodness, faith, Meekness, temperance: against such there is no law. And they that are Christ's have crucified the flesh with the affections and lusts. If we live in the Spirit, let us also walk in the Spirit*" (Galatians 5:22-25).

As we walk in the Spirit, let us also ask His help in steadfastly applying the ax to all roots of bitterness, through our repentance and forgiveness. As the Psalmist prayed, so should we on a daily basis: *"Create in me a clean heart, O God; and renew a right spirit within me"* (Psalm 51:10). Don't let Satan trip you up!

How About You?

1. Do you think forgiveness is a one-time action? Do you think it's a lack of faith to forgive more than once for the same offense?

2. Is there anyone you are still having a difficult time forgiving? Is forgiveness a feeling? What does it take to forgive?

3. What will you do if the forgiveness seems one-sided?

4. How are you hurting yourself when you hold unforgiveness in your heart? How would you feel if God held unforgiveness against you?

5. How heavy is the burden of unforgiveness? What does the Word have to say about our burdens?

Bitter or Better

Throughout this book we have looked at many people in the Word of God who were bitter. Some were bitter at other people, some at the circumstances of their lives, some due to affliction, and some due to their lack of knowledge of God's Word. Through their examples and the teaching presented in the Bible, we know that living in bitterness is like living in the Land of Torment. It has no part in that abundant life that Jesus provided for us, but offenses are going to come. We need to be prepared to respond with the faith of another Bible character, a man of great courage.

This is a young man who, from the world's standpoint, had every right to be bitter. He could have been bitter at his circumstances, bitter with his brothers, and even bitter towards God. His name is Joseph. Oh, not the Joseph who was married to Mary the mother of Jesus; although when you think of it, Jesus' stepfather could have been extremely bitter with Mary. Here he was, engaged to marry a young virgin, and she told him that she was already with child. She certainly said she had never been intimate with any man, but Joseph did not believe her at first. Would you have believed her?

When we open the door of our hearts to anger, very often a bitter spirit will come in, too. We may feel justified in our anger—but we probably wouldn't entertain the anger if we knew that bitterness was ready to bind us up. Joseph not only had the opportunity for anger, but he could very easily have been resentful. He had kept himself pure for her so that their marriage bed would be undefiled. His reputation in their small town was about to be destroyed through what he felt was her betrayal.

In those days, Joseph didn't have recourse to ask for a DNA test. Frankly, those who father children today and then don't take responsibility for their actions are applying DNA in a different way: Denial, Neglect, Abandonment. Joseph did not have any of these issues to deal with. Even before he had a visitation from the angel of the Lord assuring him that Mary was telling the truth, we read this: "*Then Joseph her husband, being a just man, and not willing to make her a public example, was minded to put her away privily*" (Matthew 1:19). Had Joseph hardened his heart and been resentful, he would have wanted her to be exposed to shame and ridicule. Thank God that Joseph had a tender heart and that the angel appeared to him to reassure him Mary was telling the truth. He then became the stepfather to the Lord Jesus Christ.

The Joseph we want to look at, though, is the Joseph from the book of Genesis. We discover in verse 3 of chapter 37, that Joseph was Jacob's favorite son. That would be fine if Joseph were also Jacob's only son, but Jacob had ten sons before Joseph was even born. Because Joseph was the favored son, his father made him a special coat—probably most familiar as "the coat of many colors." It was bad enough that he was obviously their father's favorite child, but this multi-colored robe made his older brothers see red every time Joseph came near.

The Background: A Romance
In case this is not a familiar story to you, the reason Joseph was singled

out by his father, Jacob, is that Jacob was madly in love with Rachel, the boy's mother. Here is a brief synopsis of their love story: Jacob sees Rachel at a well and it is love at first sight. He goes to her father, Laban, and wants to propose there on the spot—no lengthy engagement for this man. He had found his soul mate, his helpmeet, his other half, the little woman, etc. The only problem was that the custom of the Middle East dictated that not only were the marriages arranged, but each father made sure his oldest daughter was married before he arranged marriages for his younger daughters.

Laban's oldest daughter was not Rachel, but rather Leah. However, Jacob was so in love with Rachel that he told Laban he would serve Laban for seven years in order to have the younger daughter in marriage. He probably hoped that within seven years a marriage could be arranged and finalized for Leah. Jacob was so smitten with Rachel that the Bible tells us the seven years he worked to obtain her hand seemed as though they were just a few days. Isn't that amazing! The love bug had "bit him bad." It is sad that nowadays many marriages don't even last seven years.

The wedding day had finally arrived, and the marriage was consummated after dark. When morning came, Jacob opened his eyes only to find his bride wasn't Rachel, but Leah! Laban had tricked Jacob over the rights of the firstborn. How ironic! Sounds like Jacob was being paid back for having tricked his father years before in order to get the firstborn blessing. The Bible says what you sow you will reap, and I say "what goes around comes around." Jacob and Laban worked this out so that Jacob would be able to marry Rachel, but he would have to labor another seven years for her.

As the story continues, Leah begins to have sons, while Rachel is barren. When Rachel sees that she can't seem to have children, she gives her handmaiden to her husband so that Rachel will get credit for some sons through her handmaiden. Not to be outdone, Leah gives her handmaiden to Jacob as well, so that she can stay ahead in the race to have the most sons. On and on this goes between the two sisters and both of their handmaidens until Jacob has fathered ten sons. Then the Lord opens Rachel's womb, she conceives a child, and upon his birth names him Joseph—meaning the Lord will add. Even at that moment, Rachel knows she will have another son. *"And she called his name Joseph; and said, The Lord shall add to me another son"* (Genesis 30:24).

We can now understand Joseph being his father's favorite son. Can you imagine Jacob's joy when Joseph is born? This birth was the product of great love and devotion. After many years of trying and waiting, hoping and praying, Rachel and Jacob see the manifestation of their love for one another in this special son.

By this point in the story you have surely realized how important sons are to this culture. With excitement and anticipation, Rachel—sure that she will have another son—counts the days until she can know for certain that she is once again with child. The word of the Lord came to pass and she is once again pregnant. At the end of her pregnancy, the Bible comments that she had hard labor. (I know for sure that God used men to write the Bible. Any woman who has ever had a child, no matter what the time frame of delivery, will assure you that **all** labor is hard.)

At the time Rachel goes into this hard labor, the family has been traveling from Bethel (house of God) to Ephrath (fruitful). The midwife declares to Rachel that she shouldn't fear because God has added another son to her. Rachel names the newborn Ben-oni, son of my sorrow. Jacob then changes his son's name to Benjamin—son of my right hand. Son of my sorrow is a more accurate name initially. Rachel dies shortly after the birth and is buried in Ephrath.

Can you imagine Jacob's grief and sorrow over the loss of his beloved Rachel? We can see now why he was so close to Joseph and later became so very protective of Benjamin.

A Bitter Sibling Rivalry
Let's pick up Joseph's story at the time he turns seventeen years old.

His elderly father loved him dearly, but his brothers really hated him. They never seemed to have a kind word to say to him; in fact, they "*could not speak peaceably unto him*" (Genesis 37:4*b*). It seems safe to assume they treated him as an enemy and were very jealous. I don't want to paint a detailed picture of his childhood because the Scriptures say very little about that time of his life. Considering the complicated household he lived in, and the fact that his mother was not there to protect him, it doesn't seem as though his life could have been very joyful. We frequently hear that the damage that occurs in the life of a young child can affect them for years and years to come. Physical damage is bad enough, but the emotional damage caused by verbal abuse can linger well past childhood. If Joseph's brothers never spoke kind or even peaceable words to him, can you imagine some of the painful events of his childhood?

I think it's reasonable to assume that at times one or another of the brothers may have had to baby-sit him. I can remember times when my older brother Dirk was left to baby-sit me. He is five years my senior, so although I know that Dirk has always loved me as his little sister, there were times when I was a definite liability. If he wanted to go with his friends to the movies, he found himself either having to take me along or stuck at home watching me instead of a movie.

One memory is particularly vivid in my mind. Dirk was baby-sitting me and it was bedtime, but I didn't want to listen to him and go to bed. I wasn't even going to put my pajamas on! I just told him he would have to deal with it. Well, deal my brother did, and we ended up in a fight. On my part, I screamed at him that I would not get ready for bed. He wasn't my father and he couldn't make me go to bed. It's not hard for you to picture the result. I resisted almost to the point of bloodshed and please remember that my brother loved me. Picturing this, think for a moment of Joseph's childhood where he was outnumbered ten to one!

Psalm 105:19 says that Joseph was tested as "*the word of the Lord tried him.*" The word *tried* means to be melted and refined by the fire to separate all impurities. Joseph went through a number of tests, which we will discuss. Keep in mind, though, that after enduring all of these tests, he came through with no bitterness. Joseph turned out better, not bitter—in spite of his brothers. We're going to find that Joseph never displayed anger or resentment, but rather the love of God and real forgiveness.

The first test he had to overcome was the daily mistreatment by his brothers. Okay, they were only half-brothers, but they were still family. From the passage in Genesis 37:4, we surmise that he may have had many challenges in his personal relationships with them because they hated him.

At age 17, Joseph had two dreams about his future. One dream or vision dealt with his brothers. It pictured all of them binding sheaves in the field. Joseph's sheaf rose up and his brothers' sheaves then bowed to his sheaf. The other dream concerned his father, mother, and eleven brothers bowing down to him in the form of the sun and moon and eleven stars. Due to his youth and inexperience—in my opinion—he ran to tell his brothers his first dream. You can just imagine how well that dream went over with them. "...*They hated him yet the more for his dreams, and for his words*" (Genesis 37:8). Most of us won't have dreams of such preferential treatment, but we still may have goals for our future. How hard it is not to get bitter when we have received a dream, vision, or a goal for our future, and our families don't show any support. As a matter of fact, Joseph's brothers were completely hostile towards him. Genesis 37:11 says "*and his brethren envied him....*" Envy and jealousy can lead people to do some terrible things.

Jacob sent Joseph to see how his other sons were doing in the field and how the flocks were. On his way, Joseph met a man who told him that his brothers were in Dothan. The brothers saw him coming and conspired to kill him. One brother was the only dissenter, but he convinced the others that it would be more profitable to sell Joseph into slavery. Can you imagine such betrayal from your own relatives? They stored Joseph in a handy pit and waited for slave traders to come by.

Severe Testing

This was actually only the beginning of a downward spiral for poor Joseph. Some Midianite slave traders bought him from his brothers, took him with them to Egypt, and then sold him to Potiphar. It is particularly interesting that the name *Midianite* means "conflict, contention, and confusion."[1] Seems to me that Joseph's brothers were the real Midianites; they had conflict and contention all along with Joseph. I also think that at this point in his life, Joseph could really relate to the confusion part. What had he done to be treated as a hostage? Would his dad rescue him? Why had God allowed this to happen?

Wouldn't Joseph be tempted to be bitter? The Bible tells us, however, that in Potiphar's house, the Lord was with Joseph, and Joseph was elevated to the position of head servant with everything under his control. When the Lord is with you, it seems that even unbelievers will trust you, and the implication is that Joseph was not harboring bitterness. Instead, God *"blessed the Egyptian's house for Joseph's sake; and the blessing of the Lord was upon all that he had in the house, and in the field"* (Genesis 39:5b).

The next act in the drama of Joseph's life involved a new villain who definitely couldn't be trusted: Potiphar's wife. She began to try to seduce Joseph. Just when everything seemed to be going well for him, too. Joseph wouldn't give in to her sexual advances because he reminded her of how much his master trusted him. *"How then can I do this great wickedness, and sin against God?"* he asked her.

She didn't think much of his question, not knowing Joseph or his God. She continued to tempt him to lie with her. One day they ended up alone. (Hmm! Wonder how that happened?) She put the move on Joe, but Joseph had some moves of his own and sprinted out of the house, leaving his coat in her hands. You probably are familiar with the saying about the fury of a woman who has been scorned. Potiphar's wife called to the men of her house and accused Joseph of trying to rape her. Potiphar had no choice but to put Joseph in prison.

Surely Joseph was bitter about this new circumstance. He was imprisoned for doing what was right! The Bible tells us that though Joseph was falsely accused and condemned without a trial, even in prison the Lord was with Joseph. If the Lord was there, you can be sure Joseph was not holding on to bitterness. Because of God's blessing on Joseph, he gained favor with those in charge of the prison and became the warden over his cell block.

One day two new prisoners arrived: the cupbearer for the king and the royal chief baker. They had somehow offended Pharaoh. These two servants continued in prison for a time and Joseph ministered to them. One morning they both looked so sad that Joseph asked what was troubling them. Both men had dreamed some puzzling dreams the night before and wanted the interpretations of these dreams. (Hmm again.) Hadn't it been the interpretation of a dream or two that had escalated the problems in Joseph's personal life? Surely he was tempted to just walk away. But no, Joseph allowed God to use him to interpret their dreams. The men told him their dreams and Joseph supplied the following interpretations to them: In three days the cupbearer would be released, and in three days the baker would be deceased.

Joseph told the cupbearer, "*But think on me when it shall be well with thee, and shew kindness, I pray thee, unto me, and make mention of me unto Pharaoh, and bring me out of this house*" (Genesis 40:14). Joseph went on to say that he was an innocent man and didn't deserve to be incarcerated. "*For indeed I was stolen away out of the land of the Hebrews: and here also have I done nothing that they should put me into the dungeon*" (Genesis 40:15). Both dreams were fulfilled: the cupbearer was freed and the baker was executed. Don't you think after the cupbearer's release that Joseph was waiting daily with bated breath to hear the footsteps of the guards coming to release him, too? But once again he was forgotten—not for a day, a week, a month, or a year, but for two years more of captivity. Is there reason here for Joseph to gradually become bitter at both God and the cupbearer? Yes. Did Joseph become bitter? No. He had <u>faith</u> that God had a better plan.

Fulfillment of Other Dreams

Finally, the King of Egypt has two dreams that none of his wise men can interpret. Our forgetful cupbearer remembers Joseph—because of the similarity of circumstance, I suppose—and tells the King of the young man he had "done time with." Without any further delay, the guards are on the way to release Joseph.

After thirteen years of injustice, Joseph is taken out of the dungeon and brought before the ruler of all Egypt to interpret Pharaoh's dreams. After he explains the visions and dreams, one of his own dreams becomes reality. Joseph goes from the pit to the palace in a moment's time. God raises this worthy young man to the position of prime minister in Egypt.

Joseph had been only seventeen when his brothers sold him into slavery. Now he's a grown man, thirty years old. Pharaoh puts incredible power into his hands: "*And Pharaoh said unto Joseph, I am Pharaoh, and without thee shall no man lift up his hand or foot in all the land of Egypt*" (Genesis 41:44). He also arranges a marriage for Joseph with Asenath, the daughter of the priest of On (v.45) and they have two sons. (v. 46,50).

In a previous chapter we looked at the names Joseph had given his two sons. For our purposes in seeing Joseph's lack of bitterness, we should look again at the testimony of the names. "*And Joseph called the name of the firstborn Manasseh: For God, said he, hath made me forget all my toil, and all my father's house. And the name of the second called he Ephraim: For God hath caused me to be fruitful in the land of my affliction*" (Genesis 41:51,52). The only way to recover from bitterness is to ask God to cause us to forget the pain and to make us fruitful *even in and through our afflictions*. So often we would like to think that prosperity is a sign that we are truly walking with God. Doesn't He want us to live pain-free lives? *We* want us to live pain-free lives, but the Bible stresses over and over and over again that we are refined, tested, and proven in times of trial and affliction. Is that what God desires for us—affliction? No, but it *is* the way we learn. That's just a fact.

Seven years of plenty come as Joseph prophesied from Pharaoh's dream. Then the seven years of famine finally hit. This is a widespread famine, and affects Jacob and Joseph's brothers such that Jacob sends the boys to Egypt to buy food and provisions. Well, guess who's "the man" in the land! The brothers approach this ruler, whom they don't recognize since it's been twenty years since baby brother was booted from the homeland. They bow before him, thus fulfilling the vision Joseph had in his youth.

Joseph provides food for his brothers, but keeps his identity under wraps. He sends most of them home, retaining one brother as a hostage so that they will return later with Benjamin in tow. He also provides some interesting tests for them along the way. He hides money in their sacks of grain; hadn't they sold him for money? Would they return the money? Joseph later has his servants hide his own cup in one of the grain sacks. He was forgotten by the cupbearer, was he also forgotten by his brothers? A resolution to this situation is on the way... Joseph knows full well that the famine will last long enough that his brothers will have to return to Egypt. They do, and before long, Joseph reveals himself to them as their brother. He is deeply concerned about his father and wants his whole extended family to live with him—including all of his brothers and their wives and children.

Doing Good to Those "Who Despitefully Use You"

Would that have been our first concern if we were in his shoes? I can't speak for you, the reader, but I can say that for me, vengeance and retaliation might have been more the order of the day. We can judge a man's heart by his words and his actions. Are Joseph's words ones of bitterness because of what his brothers made him suffer? Does he speak of anger and revenge? Does he try to cut his brothers "down to size"? No, because he allowed the bitter events in his life to make him a better man. Instructing them to draw near, he said this:

> *"I am Joseph your brother, whom ye sold into Egypt. Now therefore be not grieved, nor angry with yourselves, that ye sold me hither: for God did send me before you to preserve life. For these two years hath the*

*famine been in the land: and yet there are five years, in the which
there shall neither be earing nor harvest. And God sent me before you
to preserve you a posterity in the earth, and to save your lives by a great
deliverance"* (Genesis 45: 4b-7).

Can you believe the goodness of this man? He tells them not to be sad
or angry with themselves. He also tells them he plans to save them from
the famine and do good things for them. I think we need to look at verse
ten because there's a hidden key to the forgiveness. *"And thou shalt dwell
in the land of Goshen, and thou shalt be near unto me...."* When we have
released the bitterness and let the offenders go free, we want them near to
us. Many times I have forgiven, but the acid test of real forgiveness is
whether I want those I have "forgiven" near me.

For most of us, this will be an appropriate response to those who have
hurt us. I need to address briefly those of you, however, who are in abu-
sive situations. Like David with the murderous King Saul, we certainly
need to forgive the other person, but we probably need to stay away from
him or her until the pattern of abuse ends. We can minister through
praying blessings and openness to God for the other person, regardless of
where we are on the planet.

Father Jacob is reunited with Joseph as he and the brothers all live in
the land of Goshen not only throughout the rest of the famine, but for
seventeen years in all. At the end of this time, "full of years," Joseph's
father dies. The brothers once again become nervous, thinking about
their earlier betrayal of Joseph. By now it's been at least 37 years since
they sold Joseph into slavery. Thirty-seven years have gone by, and yet for
Joseph's brothers, time has stood still.

*And when Joseph's brethren saw that their father was dead, they said,
Joseph will peradventure hate us, and will certainly requite us all the
evil which we did unto him. And they sent a messenger unto Joseph,
saying, Thy father did command before he died, saying, So shall ye say
unto Joseph, Forgive, I pray thee now, the trespass of thy brethren, and*

their sin; for they did unto thee evil: and now, we pray thee, forgive the trespass of the servants of the God of thy father. And Joseph wept when they spake unto him. And his brethren also went and fell down before his face; and they said, Behold, we be thy servants. And Joseph said unto them, Fear not: for am I in the place of God? But as for you, ye thought evil against me; but God meant it unto good, to bring to pass, as it is this day, to save much people alive. Now therefore fear ye not: I will nourish you, and your little ones. And he comforted them, and spake kindly unto them (Genesis 50:15-21).

I want you to notice what his brothers told him was the command of their father. They said, "Father commanded that you forgive." Joseph wept when he heard these words. He had forgiven them years ago, and now upon the death of their father, the first thing they think of is that Joseph is going to take revenge. In essence, they are implying that all of his kindness was just an act in front of their daddy. Now that Dad is gone, they are really going to get what they deserve.

There is a truth in these verses for us today. Our Father says we must forgive. The Lord's Prayer is so familiar to us that we may not be paying real attention to what we are saying. Forgive us our debts AS WE forgive our debtors. We are promising that we will forgive those who have hurt us because we recognize that we are sinners, too.

We learned that early in Joseph's life his brothers didn't speak a peaceable word to him, but we find him speaking kindly to them and comforting them. The word *comfort* in this text means to lessen sorrow and disappointment. I feel sure that after the many years in which Joseph provided blessings for them, his brothers had some sorrow over what they had done to him. I am also sure they knew their behavior was a disappointment to Jacob, their father, as well as to Joseph and Benjamin. God's Word changes hearts.

"Ye have heard that it hath been said, Thou shalt love thy neighbour, and hate thine enemy. But I say unto you, Love your enemies, bless them that curse you, do good to them that hate you, and pray for

174

them which despitefully use you, and persecute you; That ye may be
the children of your Father which is in heaven: for he maketh his sun
to rise on the evil and on the good, and sendeth rain on the just and
on the unjust. For if ye love them which love you, what reward have
ye? do not even the publicans the same? And if ye salute your brethren
only, what do ye more than others? do not even the publicans so? Be ye
therefore perfect, even as your Father which is in heaven is perfect"
(Matthew 5:43-48).

These are some very difficult verses for us. However, Jesus wouldn't
give us these instructions if there were no way we could follow them.
Sometimes it seems impossible to live according to the Book, but with
God all things are possible to him who believes. Joseph believed and God
worked strongly in his life, giving him such grace to be obedient that no
one in the Old Testament seems more clearly like Jesus than Joseph does.
I've made a list of similarities between our Lord and Joseph.

1. Miraculous birth	Genesis 30:22		Matthew 1:18
2. Well-beloved, firstborn son	Genesis 37:3		Matthew 3:17
3. Lived in fellowship with father before being sent to brothers	Genesis 37:14		John 17:5,8
4. "Brothers" plotted against him	Genesis 37:19,20		Luke 19:47
5. Betrayed due to envy	Genesis 37:11		Mark 15:10
6. Sold for silver	Genesis 37:26-28	Matthew 26:15
7. Didn't sin when tempted	Genesis 39:9		Matthew 4:1-11
8. Wrongfully accused; lied about	Genesis 39:13-18	Matthew 26:59,60
9. Put in a place of "death"	Genesis 39:20		Mark 15:27
10. With two malefactors	Genesis 40:2,3		Luke 23:33
11. One lived, one died	Genesis 40:21,22	Luke 23:39-43
12. At age 30 entered "public ministry"	Genesis 41:46		Luke 3:23
13. Took a Gentile bride	Genesis 41:45	Ephesians 5:23-32
14. Savior	Genesis 47:25		1 John 4:14
15. Freely forgave	Genesis 50:21		Luke 23:34
16. Gave children an inheritance	Genesis 48:6		1 Peter 1:3,4

In comparing Joseph and Jesus, we are certainly aware of differences as well as similarities. Jesus is the Son of God. His very name speaks of His appointed purpose: *"And she shall bring forth a son, and thou shalt call his name JESUS: for he shall save his people from their sins"* (Matthew 1:21). When we, with the help of the Holy Spirit, uncover bitter roots in our heart—roots involving resentment and unforgiveness toward others as well as ourselves—we must remember the Name above all names: Jesus. If we turn to Him, He will forgive us our sins and cleanse us from all unrighteousness. What wonderful good news!

Remember that the name *Joseph* means "to add to" or "to increase." It is my prayer that the Lord will add to and increase in each of us the capacity to forgive, to release, and not to relive the offenses. May the Holy Spirit overshadow us as He did Mary and birth in us His *nature*, a nature of mercy, love, and forgiveness.

May you and I say as Mary did, *"Be it done unto me according to thy Word."*

How About You?

1. Have you ever been hurt because of something a family member did? Do you think the whole family suffered because of your wound?

2. Did your parents have favorites among the children? How can you let go of the hurts that favoritism produces?

3. What will you do the next time someone mistreats you?

4. How do you handle being disappointed? Being forgotten?

5. If given the opportunity to repay your enemy, will you be able to pray for your enemy or will you give in to the temptation for revenge? How can you prepare right now to keep yourself from being offended? (Becoming a hermit is not an option!)

6. Like Joseph, do you have a dream from God?

End Notes

1. *The Exhaustive Dictionary of Bible Names* by Dr. Judson Cornwall and Dr. Stelman Smith.

Chapter 12

Plague in the Place

Here we are at the last chapter and we're talking about a plague in the place? A plague sounds pretty serious. Yes, this is something we need to consider in order to keep our hearts free and clear of bitterness forever. I pray that the information I have shared thus far has been as life-changing for you as it has been for me. Daily we need to ask the Holy Spirit to search our hearts and convict us of sin. He will be more than faithful to do His part. But we need to look now at a bigger picture of cleansing than we have seen just yet.

Because the teaching for this chapter comes from Leviticus chapter 14, you need to pause in your reading of this book and pick up your favorite Bible. Read chapter 14 so that you'll know the story, and then come back and we'll study the teaching piece by piece. No cheating. Read the chapter all the way through.

*   *   *   *

The first thirty-two verses of chapter 14 deal with the cleansing of a person who has leprosy. Leprosy was often used in the Bible as a symbol for sin, so we could liken the person suffering leprosy to ourselves when we are harboring bitterness. One of the interesting things about leprosy is that it attacks the nerve-endings and causes them to be desensitized. That might sound like a good thing at first—Hey, Mom, no pain!—but without the nerves telling us when we are being hurt, we end up damaging ourselves, sometimes irreparably, without even knowing it.

Bitterness can have a similar effect. If we cling to our unforgiveness and our anger, we desensitize ourselves to the things of God. Focused on the wrong things entirely, we damage our spiritual nature terribly, and we don't look too attractive in the process, either. The initial stages of leprosy and bitterness may be easy to hide, but a full-blown case is impossible to miss. Fellowship is broken with those we love and we isolate ourselves in our uncleanness and our hurt.

Although the instructions in chapter 14 of Leviticus are very specific as far as the cleansing for someone healed of leprosy, I can't find any recorded case of someone being healed—except for Miriam and Naaman—until Jesus healed the leper:

> And behold, a leper came up to Him and, prostrating himself, worshiped Him, saying, Lord, if You are willing, You are able to cleanse me by curing me. And He reached out His hand and touched him, saying, I am willing; be cleansed by being cured. And instantly his leprosy was cured and cleansed. And Jesus said to him, See that you tell nothing about this to anyone; but go, show yourself to the priest and present the offering that Moses commanded, for a testimony [to your healing] and as an evidence to the people. [Leviticus 14:2.] (Matthew 8:2-4, Amplified Version).

Do you suppose that the instructions given to Moses were just for this time over a thousand years later when Jesus would heal a leper? Jesus cleanses us as well, when we ask Him to cure us of our sins. Leviticus 14:1-32 deals with individuals with leprosy, but there is another kind of breakout of leprosy that we must examine in order to keep our lives free of bitterness.

Leprosy in the House?

Let's look at Leviticus 14:33. This section describes housecleaning from a unique perspective: how to clean your house when there's an infection or a disease in the house itself. Did you ever hear a teaching on this chapter? I hadn't until God started to speak to me personally, telling me there was a plague in my house. At first, I didn't have a clue as to what He meant, so I started searching through the Scriptures and sure enough— I found this story in Leviticus. (By the way, if you're reading the New International Version and are wondering what I've been talking about, the NIV translates the word *leprosy* as *mildew* when referring to houses.)

We should cover a little historical background before we actually study the verses. When the children of Israel came into the land of Canaan, the Hittites and the Amorites and all the "Ite—ites" that were living there knew that Israel was coming. They were afraid of the Israelites because they had heard what happened at Jericho and Ai. The Israelites had captured these foreign towns and had taken all their spoils and possessions. How could the Canaanites protect their treasures from this God-blessed onslaught? They took their idols of gold and silver, and they hid the idols in the walls of their homes.

When the children of Israel overcame these towns, they moved in to occupy and possess what had once been owned by Canaan. All of a sudden, without any apparent reason, mildew, or leprosy, would appear on the walls. God directed them to scrape off all the green and red mildew, plaster over it, and put up other stones. If the mildew returned, they would have to break down the infected house. As they tore down the infected house, starting with the leprous area, they would find the little foreign gods hidden in the walls.

God wants a clean house, and this isn't just our physical house or temple. All of us at one time were involved in some form of idolatry. We might not have worshiped golden calves, but we have all chosen to worship other things besides the Creator. Every now and then we'll have a little spiritual mildew or leprosy break out in our "homes." God is serious about us getting our homes clean, as we can see from the instructions in chapter 14 of Leviticus. In order for us to see the direct connection to our spiritual lives, I'm going to break these cleaning directions down to six steps.

In verse 35 we see that at the first awareness of a plague or uncleanness in the home, <u>step one is to tell the priest</u>: "*Then he who owns the house shall come and tell the priest, It seems to me there is some sort of disease in my house*" (Amplified Bible). The first thing we need to do as children of God is to tell the *priest* of the problem in the home. Usually we tell each other instead. We share with our friends the trouble we are having with our children and our marriages, when we should be telling Jesus, our High Priest. In fact, we go to anyone and everyone that will listen to us. (That deserves an "Amen, Sister Gwen!" because you know I'm telling the truth!)

We want a tangible person to sit down and have coffee with and discuss our problems. We call our friends and ask them to come over to talk and pray with us. So we talk and sometimes we pray, but mostly we end up talking more than we pray. When this happens, the problem gets magnified—whether it's the rebellious children or the unsaved husband we're discussing. It took me a long time to learn that when I have a problem in my home—whether it's me, my children, my husband, or my attitude—the first thing I need to do is go to the Priest. I was saved for a long time before I realized that I was going to everyone but God. He was the last person I cried out to.

I'm not saying it's wrong to have a prayer partner. We need each other. But when your home is in trouble, you need to go first to Jesus. He is the Priest who ever lives to intercede for us at the right hand of God, and I'm a living witness that there is no problem in any of our homes that Jesus can't heal. "*But this man [Jesus], because he continueth ever, hath an un-*

changeable priesthood. Wherefore he is able also to save them to the uttermost that come unto God by him, seeing he ever liveth to make intercession for them" (Hebrews 7:24,25). *"For we have not an high priest which cannot be touched with the feeling of our infirmities; but was in all points tempted like as we are, yet without sin"* (Hebrews 4:15). I'm so glad that what touches me touches Jesus. Aren't you? First, go tell the Priest: Jesus.

At the Priest's Command

The second step and third step are closely tied together. Step two is to examine the house and step three is to cleanse it. Instructions are found in verses 36-38 for us to empty and examine the house. This comes at the priest's command. Remember the story in Exodus of the very first Passover? God told the Israelites He would deliver them from their bondage in Egypt, but there were certain things they needed to do first. One direction He gave was to search the house for leaven. (See Exodus 12.) Leaven in the Bible represents sin and hypocrisy. Every scrap had to be out of the house. Nowadays, Jewish families who celebrate Passover remove all the leaven from their homes except for one piece of leavened bread, which they hide. It is the children's job to take a flashlight and find the hidden leaven. They also take with them a wooden spoon and a feather because they don't want to touch the leaven; they don't want to touch sin. When they find the leaven, they shine the light on it, and with the feather they sweep the leaven onto the wooden spoon. Then they run to their father saying, "Father, here's the leaven." It is the father's job to get the leaven out of the house. Aren't you glad that we have a Father who still wants to take care of hidden leaven in our lives, things we aren't even aware are there?

A friend of mine, Thelma, loved the Lord and was saved but couldn't seem to praise Him or pray in the trailer she lived in. Her trailer was very cute, and was suitable for a single, widowed woman, but she just couldn't get a prayer or praise breakthrough when she was there. This was odd because when she went anywhere else, she had no hindrance in her prayers.

One day, she invited me over for tea. As soon as I walked into her house, I sensed that something was not right. God does equip us with discernment, and sometimes it can come in the form of our feeling very uncomfortable. Things may look right and sound right, but the Spirit tells us that something isn't right. I sat down in Thelma's house, but I kept feeling really uncomfortable. Finally, I turned and looked around me. On the wall above me was a large clock decorated with the signs of the zodiac. I knew this was not a good thing for a Christian to have, but this was years ago and I was less bold than I am now. I kept thinking to myself, "You know, Gwen, it's not your place to tell her about this clock."

I didn't say anything about it to Thelma, but the thought of the whole thing bothered me for two weeks. Time went by, and she invited me back again. When I entered her trailer she began sharing with me the trouble she was having praying and praising in her trailer. She said, "Gwen, this is my home. If there's any place I ought to be able to pray, it's my home."

I thought for a moment and then answered her, "Thelma, you may become offended with this, but I have to tell you something. That clock on the wall is really offensive to the Holy Spirit. The symbols on it are symbols of the world, demonic activity, and the occult. I believe the clock is what is hindering your worship."

Thelma hollered at me, "Why didn't you tell me before? You should have told me the first day you walked into my house!. How dare you not tell me!" With this, seventy-year old Thelma jumped up and went to the shed in back of her trailer. She came back swinging a hammer! Frankly, I was scared to death. She yelled, "Get that off the wall!"

I meekly answered, "Yes, Ma'am," and I took that huge clock down and carried it out of her house. Thelma put a trash can in her driveway and then beat that clock to smithereens. Plaster may have been flying in all directions, but do you know what the real outcome was? She has never since been hindered in her prayer and praise in her home.

Sometimes when we find out that there are items in our homes that are problems, we want to sell them or give them away. We can't bring ourselves to destroy something that would have value to someone else. Let me tell you what happened in Ephesus when the Jews and Greeks there were convinced that Jesus was Lord. *"Many of them also which used curious arts brought their books together, and burned them before all men: and they counted the price of them, and found it fifty thousand pieces of silver"* (Acts 19:19). The very next verse tells the result of their cleansing: *"So mightily grew the word of God and prevailed"* (v.20).

I was once given a little golden ram with horns by a pastor's wife who had been traveling in Africa. As soon as she put it in my hand, I knew something was wrong. I felt badly because she had planned it as a gift for me, but I knew I couldn't keep it. Part of my reluctance to get rid of it, though, stemmed from the fact that it was solid gold. I thought about praying over it, melting it down, and making a bracelet out of it. Perhaps I could anoint it with oil…. But God told me, "No." I had to get rid of it.

Ten years later, God told me, "I want you to clean out your bookshelf." I knew He meant something other than the dust, the dirt, and the fuzz bunnies, so I took everything off that shelf. Between a couple of magazines I found a book that a Jehovah's Witness had given me years earlier. I got rid of it because God said, "I want this house clean."

It's important to be careful what comes into your home, but don't go to the extreme of becoming legalistic either. The blood of Jesus is powerful in sanctifying us, and God will be faithful to direct you personally.

If you are a parent, you are responsible, too, for what your children bring into your home. We wouldn't let our children put up posters that were offensive. Whether they liked it or not, it was our house. Their bedrooms were their own, but those rooms were located in our house. We have to be careful to keep the house clean. <u>When we pray—when we really pray—the Lord will reveal if something should not be in the house.</u> The Priest says, "I want you to examine the house. Empty it, examine it, and bring out of the house anything that's not godly." You can pray all you want for the Lord to visit you in your home, but if you have things that offend Him, His presence may not be as strong and as intimate as it could be. Step two: empty and examine. Step three: Cleanse.

Being Watchful

The fourth step is to watch out for break out. *"And if the plague come again, and break out in the house, after that he hath taken away the stones, and after he hath scraped the house, and after it is plastered; Then the priest shall come and look, and, behold, if the plague be spread in the house, it is a fretting leprosy in the house: it is unclean"* (Leviticus 14:43,44). When I first read these verses I had no idea what a fretting leprosy was. The language of the King James Bible is sometimes hard to understand, so I had to look up all the words. Let me back up a bit and paraphrase in modern day language. The priest went in and examined the house, and the occupants cleansed the house: they scrubbed the mildew off the wall, they cloroxed it, and they sprayed room freshener so that everything was nice and clean. Unfortunately, at this point we have a tendency to sit back and think all is going to stay well. In verse 43 and 44 we find out that the plague could come back.

When I looked up "fretting leprosy" I found that other translations said "malignant or destructive plague," "destructive mildew," or "active mildew." These are all words that talk about great damage taking place. Searching a bit further, I found that the Hebrew word used for fretting is *mara.* Yes, this is the same word we began with. Mara means bitterness. It is bitterness that we need to guard against in our home on a daily basis. We need to be watchful that there is no breakout of bitterness. If we are offended by family members or neighbors or whoever, we need to deal right away with that offense. Otherwise, we end up swallowing that mara, and the bitter thing begins to dwell in our home. It might be weeks, it might be months, it might take years, but I'm telling you that bitterness will break out somewhere.

So often as believers we think we shouldn't be offended; however, when we suffer an offense, we keep swallowing the bitterness and saying, "I forgive" and "I don't hold any offense" *without really dealing with the issue in our hearts*. At the same time, this breakout is destroying our homes. It's malignant, it's active, it's living, and it's a killer. I want us to be able to say to Jesus, "I have no bitterness in my heart at all for You to put up with because I've been watching out for the spreading leprosy and scraping it off the wall of my heart. I am going to tear down and re-plaster every wall every day if I have to for the rest of my life. I have chosen not to be bitter."

The fifth step is to cleanse yourself.
"Moreover he that goeth into the house all the while that it is shut up shall be unclean until the even. And he that lieth in the house shall wash his clothes; and he that eateth in the house shall wash his clothes. And if the priest shall come in, and look upon it, and, behold, the plague hath not spread in the house, after the house was plastered: then the priest shall pronounce the house clean, because the plague is healed" (Leviticus 14:46-48).

We need to watch out for breakout, but we have to cleanse ourselves. We have to stop blaming everyone else. It doesn't matter what anyone else did to us or how we suffered because in the end, we individually need to come clean before God.

"Having therefore these promises, dearly beloved, let us cleanse ourselves from all filthiness of the flesh and spirit, perfecting holiness in the fear of God" (2 Corinthians 7:1). When is the last time you did some real cleansing and repentance? One good thing about my Roman Catholic upbringing was that I was taught the importance of confession. We can't just let sin go and pile up in our lives. We can't come to God or partake of communion if we are holding onto sins in our lives. Every night I ask the Lord, "Have I done anything today that's not pleasing in Your sight?" Believe me, God is faithful to answer that question. I usually find myself taking inventory of the day and thinking, "You know, Lord, I'm sorry about this" or "I could have handled that better" or "I should have been nicer to that person," and "Lord, I really had an attitude that was wrong."

God is faithful and just to cleanse us of all unrighteousness when we confess our sins and ask for His forgiveness.

When I was a child, I prayed as a child:

Now I lay me down to sleep
I pray the Lord my soul to keep
And should I die before I wake
I pray the Lord my soul to take.

Believe me, I'm not confessing my sins because I'm afraid I'll die after falling asleep. I'm worried about not being clean before a holy God. I want to be able to follow step five, having cleansed myself through confession so that my High Priest, Jesus, will be able to say, "The plague is gone and the house is clean."

Atonement: Old Testament and New

Step six comes from verses 49-53 of this passage and involves making atonement so the house will be clean. Everyone of us needs to make sure that we have atonement for our homes. In the Word, this involves a ceremony. Let's assume we've already gone through the steps of telling Jesus, our Priest, that we have a problem; examining the problem to make sure we're not the cause or root of the problem; then cleansing our house; watching out for hidden bitterness that might cause a breakout; and cleaning ourselves through confession and receiving forgiveness. Then we will ask for atonement.

> And he shall take to cleanse the house two birds, and cedar wood, and scarlet, and hyssop: And he shall kill the one of the birds in an earthen vessel over running water: And he shall take the cedar wood, and the hyssop, and the scarlet, and the living bird, and dip them in the blood of the slain bird, and in the running water, and sprinkle the house seven times: And he shall cleanse the house with the blood of the bird, and with the running water, and with the living bird, and with the

cedar wood, and with the hyssop, and with the scarlet: But he shall let go the living bird out of the city into the open fields, and make an atonement for the house: and it shall be clean (Leviticus 14:49-53).

(By the way, if you look at Leviticus 14:1-6, you'll notice that the same instructions are given for cleansing the leper as for cleansing the leprous or mildewed house.)

The first item I want to look at in this ceremony is the earthen vessel. Another place in Scripture where earthen vessels are mentioned is 2 Corinthians 4:7. *"But we have this treasure in earthen vessels, that the excellency of the power may be of God, and not of us."* In the case of the leprous house, the earthen vessel is filled with clean water. Then the priest takes two sacrificial birds, which are alive and clean. He takes a piece of cedarwood and places one of the birds on the wood. A hyssop branch is laid on top of the bird and the whole thing is wrapped with scarlet thread, fastening the bird to the cedar and the hyssop. Next, the priest kills the other bird and drains the blood into the earthen vessel, which has the water in it. What's in the earthen vessel then? Blood and water. The living bird, which is lying on the cedarwood is dipped in the blood and water. Once it emerges from the mixture, the priest loosens the scarlet thread and lets the bird go free.

Obviously there is a good deal of symbolism here that relates directly the crucifixion. Cedarwood is always used in the purification rituals of a leper or even for one infected by sin. (Read Numbers 19.) The Word has a lot to say about repeated cleansings. Although we have been saved by Jesus' atonement for us, we do need daily cleansing. I was definitely saved in 1974, but unless I go to God on a daily basis, I can get pretty polluted. We still live in the world, though we're not of the world.

Cedarwood was also used to build royal palaces for kings. David used cedarwood in his home (2 Samuel 5:11), as did Solomon for his own house (1 Kings 7:2,3) and for the house of the Lord (1 Kings 5:2-6). In fact, the inner court of the temple of God was laid over with cedar beams as well. "*And above were costly stones, after the measures of hewed stones, and cedars. And the great court round about was with three rows of hewed stones, and a row of cedar beams, both for the inner court of the house of the Lord, and for the porch of the house*" (1 Kings 7:11,12). Add to this the reference to cedars in Psalm 104:16, "*The trees of the Lord are full of sap; the cedars of Lebanon, which he hath planted,*" and another picture comes to mind. Could there be a connection here between the tree of the Lord, the cross, and the trees of the Lord, the cedars? It's an interesting possibility. There are very few trees that grow in the region of the Middle East, and the cedar is one of the largest of these trees. In any event, we have seen that the cedar was used to purify anyone or anything that was unclean and was also used in housing royalty. We see a symbolic connection in that Jesus purifies us of our uncleanness and He is the King of kings.

Applying the Blood

Probably all of us have seen *The Ten Commandments* with Charlton Heston, excuse me, *Moses* leading the people out. We've seen the children of Israel on the night of the Passover, everyone gathered in the home and partaking of the sacrificial lamb. Remember that they put the blood of the lamb on the outside of the house—on the doorposts. The lamb was inside the house—and eventually inside the children of Israel as they ate the lamb. I'm here to tell you that if we can get the blood of Jesus on the outside and the Lamb of God on the inside, no matter what happens, we can be delivered.

Going back to the instructions for cleansing, the first time hyssop is mentioned in the Bible is in Exodus 12.

> *And ye shall take a bunch of hyssop, and dip it in the blood that is in the basin, and strike the lintel and the two side posts with the blood that is in the basin; and none of you shall go out at the door of his house until the morning. For the Lord will pass through to smite the Egyptians; and when he seeth the blood upon the lintel, and on the two side posts, the Lord will pass over the door, and will not suffer the destroyer to come in unto your houses to smite you* (verse 22).

The first time hyssop is mentioned, it is connected with the blood of the Lamb of God. Do you remember where hyssop appears for the last time in the Bible? It's in John 19 when Jesus is being crucified, and He says, *"I thirst."* *"Now there was set a vessel full of vinegar: and they filled a sponge with vinegar, and put it upon hyssop, and put it to his mouth. When Jesus therefore had received the vinegar, he said, It is finished: and he bowed his head, and gave up the ghost"* (John 19:29,30). Glory to God! Hyssop points us to our cleansing by the blood of the Lamb. It is interesting that the psalmist wrote of this as well in Psalm 51, *"Purge me with hyssop, and I shall be clean: wash me, and I shall be whiter than snow"* (verse 7).

So we need the cedar wood, we need Calvary, we need the cross on a daily basis to make us clean. We also need to know that no matter what happens to us, what we do, or what comes into our home, or what the enemy tries to afflict us with, if we go to Jesus we will be made clean. He's got hyssop and He can sprinkle the blood over the doors of our homes, and our homes can be made clean.

How about the scarlet thread? Scarlet definitely is used to show severity of sin: *"Though your sins be as scarlet, they shall be as white as snow; though they be red like crimson, they shall be as wool"* (Isaiah 1:18b). In Matthew 27:28 we find that as the soldiers mocked Him, they put a scarlet robe on Him. *"For he hath made him to be sin for us, who knew no sin; that we might be made the righteousness of God in him"* (2 Corinthians 5:21). The scarlet also represents the suffering of Jesus. All of these elements are a necessary part of our cleansing.

Looking back at Leviticus 14, we see that another part of the cleansing involved sprinkling the house seven times. In verse 7 we see the leper was sprinkled seven times, too. And what were they sprinkled with? Blood and water. John tells us, *"Who is he that overcometh the world, but he that believeth that Jesus is the Son of God? This is he that came by water and blood, even Jesus Christ; not by water only, but by water and blood. And it is the Spirit that beareth witness, because the Spirit is truth"* (1 John 5:5,6). Jesus bought us and redeemed us with the blood and water that flowed from His side.

Let's take a look at the whole instruction now. We start with an earthen vessel—which you and I are according to Scripture. A sacrifice was laid on wood with hyssop and scarlet. Blood was shed. Water was present. When the bird that would live went under the blood and water, it was loosened. Isn't this a picture of the death, burial, and resurrection of Jesus? We are the ones who are set free—free from the sin of bitterness and from the bitterness of sin.

Cleansed by the Sprinkling

How about the seven sprinklings? Where do they come in? The first sprinkling of His blood that I want to consider is found in Luke 2:21,22. This was when Jesus was eight days old and was brought into the temple for the ceremony of circumcision. This signified a blood covenant, setting Him apart as being dedicated to God.

The second sprinkling that involves a covenant is in Luke 22:44. "*And being in an agony he prayed more earnestly: and his sweat was as it were great drops of blood falling down to the ground.*" I take this to be literal drops of blood. What effort was involved in this prayer! He learned obedience through what He suffered and He lined up His will with the Father's will, covenanting during that night in the Garden of Gethsemane to obey the Father, even in this.

The third sprinkling comes in John 19:1. "*Then Pilate therefore took Jesus, and scourged him.*" This was to fulfill a prophecy which we will examine later. This third sprinkling is closely aligned with the fourth sprinkling, which is found in John 19:2. "*And the soldiers plaited a crown of thorns, and put it on his head....*"

Growing up in a Roman Catholic household, I can tell you that we had a crucifix in each bedroom, above each bed. I remember as a little girl, taking the crucifix down that was above my bed and laying it on my two pillows. I really looked at the image of Jesus on the cross with His crown of thorns. Even though I was a very little girl, I knew this wasn't Jesus but a representation of Him. Yet, seeing that picture of suffering, I cried and cried and cried. I remember rocking that crucifix as though it were a doll. I didn't understand then why "they" had done that to Him. But today I know why. I know why the thorns went all around His brow and were so pressed into His head that He was covered with blood. Isaiah 52 says that His image was so marred He didn't even look like a man. He suffered all of that because I put him there all by myself. My sins required a blood atonement, and Jesus willingly suffered and died to provide that atonement.

The <u>fifth sprinkling</u> occurs during the crucifixion. We actually find this specific description in the Old Testament, in Psalm 22. *"For dogs have compassed me: the assembly of the wicked have inclosed me: they pierced my hands and my feet"* (verse 16). Scholars may argue as to whether the nails went through His palms or His wrists. They may debate how big the nails were and whether they were made of lead, copper, or silver. It doesn't matter to me. What matters is His willingness to follow through with being cursed because of my sin. The Bible also says, *"Cursed is everyone that hangeth on a tree"* (Galatians 3:13; Deuteronomy 21:23).

The <u>sixth sprinkling</u> occurs after Jesus had died. When the soldiers came to break the legs of the criminals, they found Jesus was already dead. The only point in breaking the legs was to hasten the death. We read in Exodus that not a bone of the Passover lamb will be broken. (See Exodus 12:46.) God fulfills all of His Word. When the soldiers thought Jesus was already dead, one thrust a spear into His side to make sure. *"But one of the soldiers with a spear pierced his side, and forthwith came there out blood and water"* (John 19:34).

Before we go on to the seventh sprinkling of blood, I'd like to share with you what these six sprinklings mean. The first was the covenant of circumcision. God had a blood covenant with Adam, but Adam sinned and the bloodline was destroyed. Jesus came as the second Adam. *"And so it is written, The first man Adam was made a living soul; the last Adam was made a quickening spirit. Howbeit that was not first which is spiritual, but that which is natural; and afterward that which is spiritual. The first man is of the earth, earthy: the second man is the Lord from heaven"* (1 Corinthians 15:45-47). Jesus came to restore the Father's perfect bloodline. We needed to have someone cut blood covenant with God who wouldn't break the covenant. The Bible tells us that more important than circumcision of the flesh is circumcision of the heart. When you were born again, the Holy Spirit cut a blood covenant in your heart so that you have a covenant with God. <u>The first sprinkling, therefore, represents coming into covenant with God.</u>

The second sprinkling, which took place in the Garden of Gethsemane, occurred as Jesus sprinkled His blood on the ground as he wept and prayed. He said, *"Father, not My will, but Thine be done."* I'm here to tell you it's hard sometimes to do God's will. It's hard to be like Jesus because in our flesh we want to retaliate, to fight back, and be just like our attacker. But God tells us, "Don't open your mouth. I'll defend you. Just hold your peace and watch the salvation of your God." All of us have to go back to that Garden and receive God's grace to be obedient. We may feel like we're bleeding, we're hurt, and we're tired, but we must get to the point of saying, "Not my will but Thine be done. <u>This second sprinkling is for obedience.</u>

The third sprinkling, involving the crown of thorns, represents the peace that Christ provides. Where was the crown of thorns? It was pressed around His head. Isaiah said, *"Thou wilt keep him in perfect peace, whose mind is stayed on thee..."* (Isaiah 26:3). This is so helpful when we are tempted to continue in the bitterness cycle of reliving our hurts. This verse in Isaiah concludes with the words *"because he trusteth in thee."* We need to receive that peace that comes from trusting in a God who has the best possible plan for our lives. We can stop and say, "<u>There's a sprinkling of the blood of Jesus for me and for my house that provides for my peace of mind.</u>"

The fourth sprinkling is provided by the many stripes Jesus took on

His back. *"Who his own self bare our sins in his own body on the tree, that we, being dead to sins, should live unto righteousness: by whose stripes ye were healed"*(1 Peter 2:24). In Isaiah 53, that great chapter prophesying the nature of the Messiah and His atonement, we read this: *"But he was wounded for our transgressions, he was bruised for our iniquities: the chastisement of our peace was upon him; and with his stripes we are healed"* (verse 5). Not only does God care about our spiritual well-being, <u>He cares about our bodies and made provision, by this fourth sprinkling, for us to have healing.</u>

The fifth sprinkling involves the piercing of His hands and His feet. When I consider this sprinkling, I think, "Father, You want my work and my walk sanctified by His precious blood." We need that sprinkling of blood over us so that we stop asking God to bless the plans we have made and start asking Him to bless us for the tasks *He* wants us to do. Know this: *"For we are his workmanship, created in Christ Jesus unto good works, which God hath before ordained that we should walk in them"* (Ephesians 2:10). I especially like the way the Amplified Bible translates this: *"For we are God's [own] handiwork (His workmanship), recreated in Christ Jesus, [born anew] that we may do those good works which God predestined (planned beforehand) for us [taking paths which He prepared ahead of time], that we should walk in them [living the good life which He prearranged and made ready for us to live]."* <u>This fifth sprinkling is for our commitment and equipping for the tasks He prepared for us.</u>

The sixth sprinkling of the blood and water from His wounded side speaks of our being born again and washed by the water of the Word. Jesus Himself said, *"Except a man be born of water and of the Spirit, he cannot enter into the kingdom of God"* (John 3:5*b*) We also read about the water and blood in 1 John.

> *This is he that came by water and blood, even Jesus Christ; not by water only, but by water and blood. And it is the Spirit that beareth witness, because the Spirit is truth. For there are three that bear record in heaven, the Father, the Word, and the Holy Ghost; and these three are one. And there are three that bear witness in earth, the spirit, and*

the water, and the blood: and these three agree in one (5:6-8).

<u>The sixth sprinkling provides us with the new birth as our sins are forgiven through the sacrifice of Christ and as we are drawn to Him. We side with Him.</u>

Now we must look at the seventh sprinkling. If you've been noticing the chronological order, you've guessed that this must occur after the resurrection of Christ. How could He sprinkle His blood at that point? We find the account in John chapter 20. Mary and some of the women came early in the morning to the tomb to anoint His body with spices, and He was gone. Mary turned, crying, from the tomb. She thought she saw the gardener and decided to ask him where the body of the Lord might be. The gardener was actually Jesus, and He called her by name. (That part is both tender and exciting to me. I can't wait for the day when I hear Him call me by name!) As soon as Mary heard Him say her name, she knew Him and said, "*Rabboni!*" Jesus, however, told her not to touch Him because He had not yet ascended to God. He further told her to inform the disciples that He would be with them after He ascended to the Father.

Mary told the disciples she had seen the Lord and gave them Jesus' message. That same evening, Jesus appeared in the midst of the disciples, showing them His hands and His side as proof. Thomas was not with them at that time, and doubted they had really seen the Lord. He declared he wouldn't believe it was really Jesus unless he could touch the wounds in His hands and feet and side. A few days later, Jesus appeared again to the disciples and told Thomas, "*Reach hither thy finger, and behold my hands; and reach hither thy hand, and thrust it into my side: and be not faithless, but believing*" (John 20:27).

This incident provokes the question, why couldn't Mary, who loved Jesus and came to worship Him and anoint His body, be allowed to touch Jesus? Why would Thomas, who doubted the reality of the Lord's appearing and was rebuked for doubting, be allowed instead to touch Him?

The answer is that the seventh sprinkling occurred in between the two encounters. This sprinkling had to be done in heaven. Jesus ascended to God and sprinkled His blood on the heavenly mercy seat. If you read Leviticus 16, which recounts the details of the Day of Atonement, the priest was not allowed behind the veil to the Ark of the Covenant and the mercy seat without the sprinkling of blood. The high priest was, in fact, supposed to sprinkle blood seven times on the mercy seat. Jesus is our High Priest. He had to go into the heavens to the original tabernacle, of which the earthly tabernacle was only a shadow, and sprinkle His blood for us on the mercy seat. <u>The seventh sprinkling made atonement for us and allows us to enter into the Holy of Holies to worship the Lord God.</u>

When we need restoration because of a break in relationship, a wounded spirit, or a grieving heart, God can provide the grace we need for reconciliation. He will deliver us and cleanse us because He loves us. Do we dare withhold our forgiveness from someone else when God has provided so perfectly and lavishly for us? *"And be ye kind one to another, tenderhearted, forgiving one another, even as God for Christ's sake hath forgiven you"* (Ephesians 4:32).

Atonement is what Jesus provided for us. Let's break that word down for a moment into these parts: At-one-ment. We are "at one-ment" with God if we've received the atonement of His blood. If we are at one with Him, there simply cannot be any room for bitterness toward one another.

I'd like to share this prayer with you.

Thank You for mercy, plain and simple. Thank You for the seven sprinklings of the precious blood of Jesus. God, seal this word to our hearts, and help us to watch carefully for any leprosy of bitterness in our lives. Give us the courage to cleanse our homes. Give us the ability to really look in the inner court and see the things that are in our hearts. Help us to be like David, saying, "Create in me a clean heart. Renew in me, O God, a right spirit. Cast me not away from Thy presence, and take not Thy Holy Spirit from me." Thank You, Jesus, for the Word You have given us and for the encouragement and the hope it provides. I pray for all of us, Lord, that our homes would be places where You would feel comfortable to dwell. Purge us from anything that would defile—especially the root of bitterness.

Thank you, Jesus!

How About You?

1. Have you personally received the benefit of the seven sprinklings Jesus provided on your behalf?

2. I have shared Ephesians 4:32 several times in this book. When you read this verse, are you convicted by the Holy Spirit concerning your attitude or behavior toward anyone? Ask for God's grace and the faith to forgive completely. Keep asking and receiving each day until the bitterness is totally gone. Bring every thought captive to Christ—especially those thoughts that are fearful or angry ones.

3. Have you hidden some of God's Word in your heart as protection from sinning? Choose several verses right now that will help keep you from holding unforgiveness or bitterness in your heart.

4. If you have been sharing this book in a Bible Study with one or more others, covenant to pray for protection for one another, that you will not fall prey to bitterness. Pray not only for a hedge of protection around marriages, family relationships, friends, pastors, and churches, but also for the mind of Christ in all things. Take courage in this: *"But we all, with open face beholding as in a glass the glory of the Lord, are changed into the same image from glory to glory, even as by the Spirit of the Lord"* (2 Corinthians 3:18). Amen!

Resources

The Bible Almanac, edited by James Packer, Merrill Tenney, and William White, Jr. , Thomas Nelson Publishers

The Complete Word Study Old Testament, Spiros Zodhiates, AMG Publishers

The Exhaustive Dictionary of Bible Names, Dr. Judson Cornwall and Dr. Stelman Smith, Bridge-Logos Publishers

Handbook on the Pentateuch, Victor P. Hamilton, Baker Books

Hebrew-Greek Key Study Bible (See Old Testament Lexical Aids), AMG Publishers

Strong's Exhaustive Concordance of the Bible, Thomas Nelson Publishers

Theological Wordbook of the Old Testament by R. Harris; Gleason Archer, Jr.; and Bruce K. Waltke

If you are interested in purchasing teaching tapes by Gwen Mouliert or in contacting her to speak at your church or conference, please call this toll-free number:
1-888-347-3946
Please visit our website at www.proclaiminghisword.org

Finally, there is one source for all your *renewal resources!*

Whether you are looking for the latest books from Iverna Tompkins, Rick Joyner or Fuchsia Pickett, or a timeless spiritual masterpiece by Smith Wigglesworth, *WindsofFire.com* has them all. *WindsofFire.com* is your one stop store for all your renewal and revival resources.

Here's what you'll discover at WindsofFire.com:

- The most banned & burned book in Christian history!
- God showed this leading Bible scholar a vision of the coming revival. Be prepared.
- The greatest Christian writer since the apostle Paul — learn about the book that sent her to prison.

- The hottest and best-selling books on the cutting edge of what God is doing on the earth today
- Life-changing messages on cassette

So visit WindsofFire.com today and find all your renewal resources

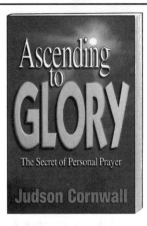

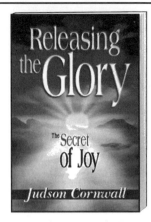

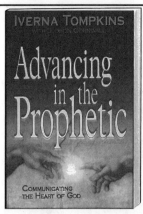

Advanced prophetic training –

This book is fresh, unique, and very insightful. You can unleash the fullness of the prophetic! You'll receive advanced prophetic training. Tompkins unearths powerful truths from the counselors in the book of Job. This book will give you fresh insight on personal prophecy and the prophetic.

You'll learn:
How to respond to prophecy
How to stir up the prophetic
How to refine truth from prophecy
How to recognize the living word in prophecy
How to reap from prophecy

Experience a fresh release of the prophetic in your life!

"Iverna has been used once again by God to bring encouragement to the body of Christ. She shows us how God uses the prophet and the prophetic word to keep us focused and to encourage us through His process."
– Jane Hansen, International President, Women's Aglow Fellowship

"Iverna Tompkins amazingly uses the life of Job to give us life-giving truths concerning prophets, prophetic ministry and God's process in perfecting His people."
– Bill Hamon, President, Christian International

Advancing in the Prophetic
by Iverna Tompkins/Judson Cornwall

ISBN: 1-883906-36-9 **Only $9.97**

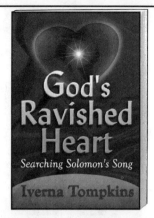

Experience pure love
as you unveil King Solomon's prophetic words!

Imagine spending the rest of your life with your true love - Jesus, the lover of your soul!

Embrace the purest love that you'll ever know and run to God with open arms. Uncover your Lord's deepest desires. Learn how He longs to spend time with you. You'll see God's heart and learn how it has been ravished by those He dearly loves! Find yourself racing into God's presence. These are heart-changing teachings!

Don't miss this fresh revelation straight from God's heart!

"God's Ravished Heart will draw you into the desire for an intimate relationship with Jesus. This is a book of love from our Bridegroom, delivered fresh to you and me. Don't miss out on the opportunity to read this timely book!"
– Alice Smith, Prayer Coordinator, U.S. Prayer Track

Like Moses and Samuel, when Iverna speaks people listen! You'll never be the same! *"When Iverna speaks, people listen - from the least to the greatest they listen. She is one of the ablest communicators of ours or any generation (she) can take a text and so exposit it that the hearer is never the same."* – Steve Fryrecording artist and author of I Am: The Unveiling of God

God's Ravished Heart
by Iverna Tompkins

ISBN: 1-883906-44-X **Only $8.97**

**Available at your local Christian bookstore
or call toll free (800) 597-1123**

Actually experience the most powerful moves of God on the earth today
through *Renewal Audio Magazine™!*

"**Renewal Audio Magazine** *will keep you at the front row of what God is doing and saying in the earth today.*"
— Bob Sorge,
Author of *The Fire of Delayed Answers*
(and many other books)

Advance to the forefront of what God is doing throughout the earth today with *Renewal Audio Magazine.*

You can experience what God is doing in your own living room, heart, and life. *Renewal Audio Magazine* harnesses the unique power of the cassette to take you where God is moving today. You'll feel God's heartbeat with an immediacy that will excite you.

Each cassette contains critical messages from some of the most anointed men and women on earth. These men and women have been specially anointed for this hour. You'll also hear exclusive interviews and much more. You'll find your spiritual

Call toll free (800) 597-1123

life moving to new levels with each cassette! *Renewal Audio Magazine* will both refresh and inspire you!

The best of Renewal Audio Magazine:

- 12 of the best audio cassette issues ever of *Renewal Audio Magazine* – hear from some of the most anointed men and women of our generation
- 12 listening guides (one for each tape)
- Deluxe storage binder stores all cassettes and listening guides
- Exclusive interviews and more
- Noted speakers include Francis Frangipane, Bob Mumford, Mike Bickle, C. Peter Wagner, Iverna Tompkins, and Ed Silvoso

Only ~~$97~~ **$87** with coupon or
special code on coupon + $9.97 shipping

60-Day Money Back Guarantee

Discover the keys to effective prayer and intercession!

Intercessors, prayer warriors, and praying Christians everywhere are discovering prayer in a fresh, powerful way. *Prayer Audio Magazine™* will catapult your prayer and intercession to new levels.

God desires to communicate intimately with you through prayer. Through *Prayer Audio Magazine* you can invite the world's leading authorities into your own home to help you pray with greater effectiveness.

Each audio cassette has been prayerfully developed to help you maximize your prayer life.

Be more effective. Be informed. Pray with greater fervency and power! Get the best of *Prayer Audio Magazine* today!

The best of Prayer Audio Magazine:

- 12 audio cassettes featuring the world's leading authorities on prayer and intercession – these are 12 of the best issues ever of *Prayer Audio Magazine*
- 12 helpful listening guides (one for each cassette)
- Deluxe storage binder stores all 12 cassettes and listening guides
- Exclusive interviews and more
- Noted speakers include: Judson Cornwall, C. Peter Wagner, and Eddie & Alice Smith

"Prayer Audio Magazine challenges us to keep pressing in to God. It keeps us informed, and brings us together to bond in prayer..."
– Pastor Jim Ottman, Maine

Only ~~$97~~ **$87** with coupon or special code on coupon + $9.97 shipping
60-Day Money Back Guarantee

Call toll free (800) 597-1123

SAVE $10

With this coupon, you can get the best of *Prayer Audio Magazine* for only **$87!**

Just mention special Code # Fire116 *to receive your $10 off!*

AMBP

1-800-597-1123   P.O. Box 486
Mansfield, PA 16933

You can experience the most enriching activity in heaven and earth!

There is no single activity which is more fulfilling or rewarding than praise. Praise is the full-time occupation of angels in heaven. The practice of praise will change your life.

This book will help you release the full experience of praise into your life. You'll by drawn into new depths of worship.

Great reading and dynamic truth that works!

"Jack Taylor's Hallelujah Factor *is not only great reading, it is dynamic truth that works! I've read it several times and find something fresh and new in it each time."* – Dr. Judson Cornwall, Leading author and worship authority

"The Hallelujah Factor is a must read for any serious worshiper..."
– Lamar Boschman,
Author and Dean of the Worship Institute

Releases fresh joy and peace!

"Seldom do I preach my way through someone else's book. The Hallelujah Factor *is an exception. This book will lead you into a lifestyle change. It will motivate you to a life of praise which results in Joy and Peace! I highly recommend it!"*
– Dr. Michael Yousseff,
Host of Leading the Way Radio

Hallelujah Factor by Jack Taylor

ISBN: 1-883906-33-4   **Only $9.97**

Code #Fire116

Discover the keys to succeeding in enemy territory!

You can not only succeed in enemy territory but you can thrive! This is your potential – you can not only win the battle for your life and mind, but tear down the fortresses of the enemy. You can truly succeed in enemy territory!

You'll learn:

How to live in victorious confidence
Five steps to resisting Satan's attacks
How to restore a broken past
How your weakest point can become your strongest
How to win the toughest battle you'll ever face

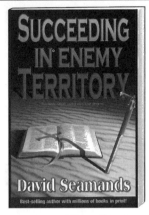

Brilliant! This book really will help you pursue your dreams!

"Succeeding in Enemy Territory, from start to finish, is a brilliant balance of personal testimony, pertinent historical illustrations, and the foundation of the Biblical drama of Joseph all working together to drive you to dream on. What a reassurance to all of us to pursue our dreams!"
– Jack Taylor, President of Dimension Ministries and author of the *Hallelujah Factor*

"This book gives new hope and encouragement..." – Dr. Norman Wright, counselor, seminar speaker, and best-selling author

Succeeding in Enemy Territory
by David Seamands

ISBN: 1-883906-34-2   **Only $9.97**

Code #Fire116

Available at your local Christian bookstore or call toll free (800) 597-1123

Fulfill the desires of your heart

God planted dreams in you for a reason – your dreams really can come true!

There is no better Biblical story for understanding the process of seeing your dreams fulfilled than the life of Joseph. Doug Murren takes you to the heart of seeing your dreams fulfilled.

This inspiring book will renew and refresh you to pursue your dreams. With *Achieving Your Dreams – The Joseph Factor*, your dreams really can come true.

 Doug has a unique ability to share truths that will change your life!

"Doug is one of today's finest young pastors/leaders and writers. He is uniquely gifted with an ability to capture the timelessness of truth and press it to the soul of today's circumstances to answer hurt or to beget hope–or both!" – Jack Hayford, Senior Pastor, The Church on the Way

A great book for all of us who dream big dreams

"The world scoffs at dreamers. God doesn't. He speaks to them. Doug Murren has written a practical, relevant book for all of us who want to dream big dreams for God and see them through." – Michele Buckingham, former Managing Editor, Ministries Today Magazine

Achieving Your Dreams by Doug Murren

ISBN: 1-883906-35-0 **Only $9.97**

Code #Fire116

How to thrive even in chaos!

Discover how you can avoid "paradigm shock"

Change is a part of life. However, shifting paradigms can make you feel overwhelmed and out of control. Whether you're a pastor, church leader, small group leader, Sunday school teacher, or other lay leader you need to be able to manage change successfully.

Learn to anticipate change, cushion transitions, and redirect focus. Find out why even crisis-initiated changes do not have to be negative.

 The experts listen to his leadership principles

"I read everything that Doug writes. Why? Because he is a pastor with an effective hand on today and a leader's eye on tomorrow. What he writes about works." – John Maxwell, Author of bestselling books including *Developing the Leader Within You*

 "...Pastor Doug Murren gives you answers you can begin to implement immediately." – C. Peter Wagner, Author and Professor of Church Growth, Fuller Theological Seminary

Leadershift by Doug Murren

ISBN: 1-883906-30-X **Only $9.97**

Code #Fire116

Available at your local Christian bookstore or call toll free (800) 597-1123

Be a more effective small group, Sunday school, or cell group leader!

Discover the nine Biblical keys that make you a more effective small group leader. You can propel small groups to new levels of fruitfulness for Christ.

Lead successful groups full of energy and life. Every small group will thrive as these scriptural keys are applied.

The Best Book on Small Groups!

"This is the best explanation in print of how God works through small groups... If I were a pastor, I would buy a copy of this book for every Sunday school teacher, small group leader, deacon, elder, staff member... every leader in my church. Then I'd buy a copy for the next set of leaders who will be produced when people get a hold of these nine keys."
– Reggie McNeal, Director of Leadership Development Team, South Carolina Baptist Convention, Columbia, SC

Carl George has been called on by congregations and leaders in 100 denominations to help them increase their effectiveness in ministry.

His writings are endorsed by leaders such as:

- **Bill Hybels**
- **Bill Bright**
- **Lyle Schaller**
- **Ralph Neighbour, Jr.**
- **Robert Coleman**
- **John Maxwell**
- **David Yonggi Cho**
- **Elmer L. Towns**

Nine Keys to Effective Small Group Leadership by Carl F. George

ISBN: 1-883906-13-X **Only $12.97**

Code #Fire116

Change Your Money Stream –

Learn why money flows to some people and away from others

 "This is the best financial teaching I've ever heard. I've used these principles for years. Finally, someone who teaches them from the Bible."
- Johnny Berguson, President of Kingdom, Inc. (Listed by *Inc. Magazine* as one of America's 500 fastest growing companies)

This is arguably the best financial book ever written. Mallonee goes to the root of finances. He explains from the Bible why money flows to some people and away from others.

Whether you have $5, $50, or $100,000, the Biblical principles in *Foolproof Finances* will work for you. These proven principles will help you get out of debt, or flourish when you're already doing well. This book will help anyone significantly improve their finances. Discover how you can be financially free.

Hardcover

Foolproof Finances by David Mallonee

ISBN: 1-883906-11-3 **Only $14.97**

Code #Fire116

Available at your local Christian bookstore or call toll free (800) 597-1123

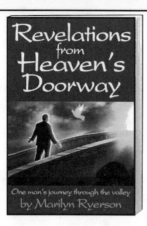
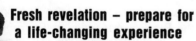
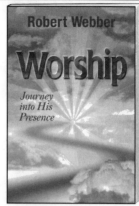